This Book Belongs To

AF519201

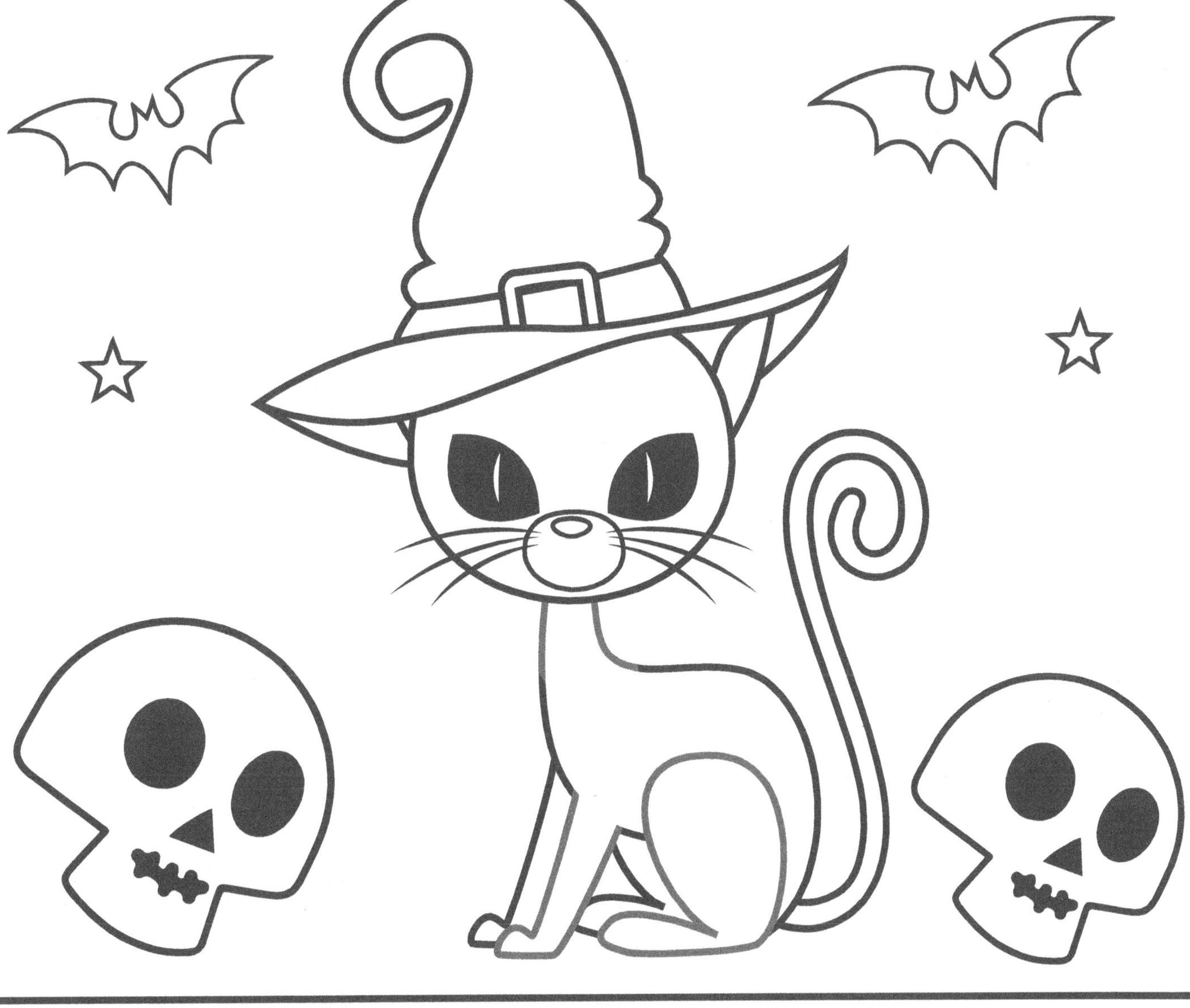

Color Test Page

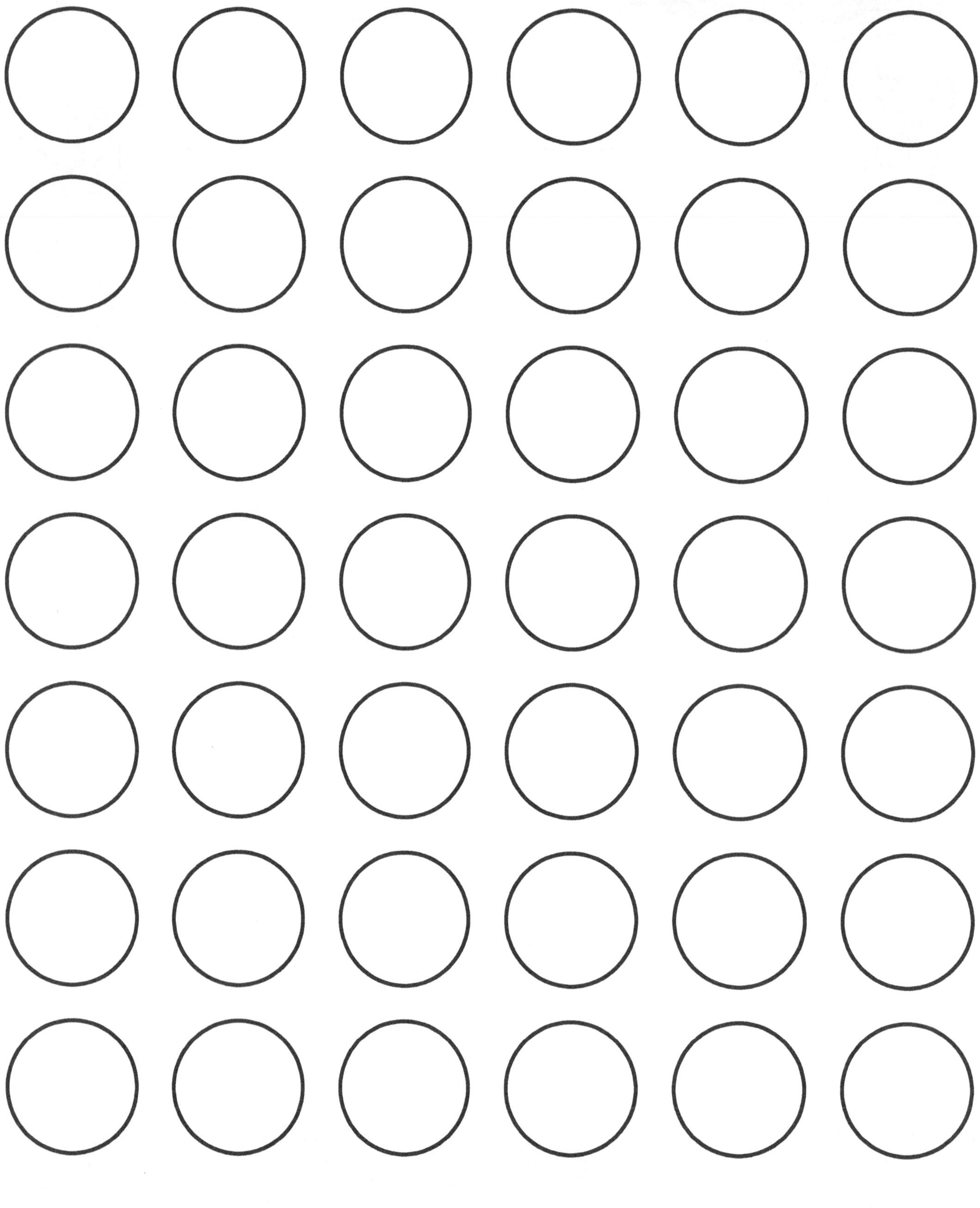

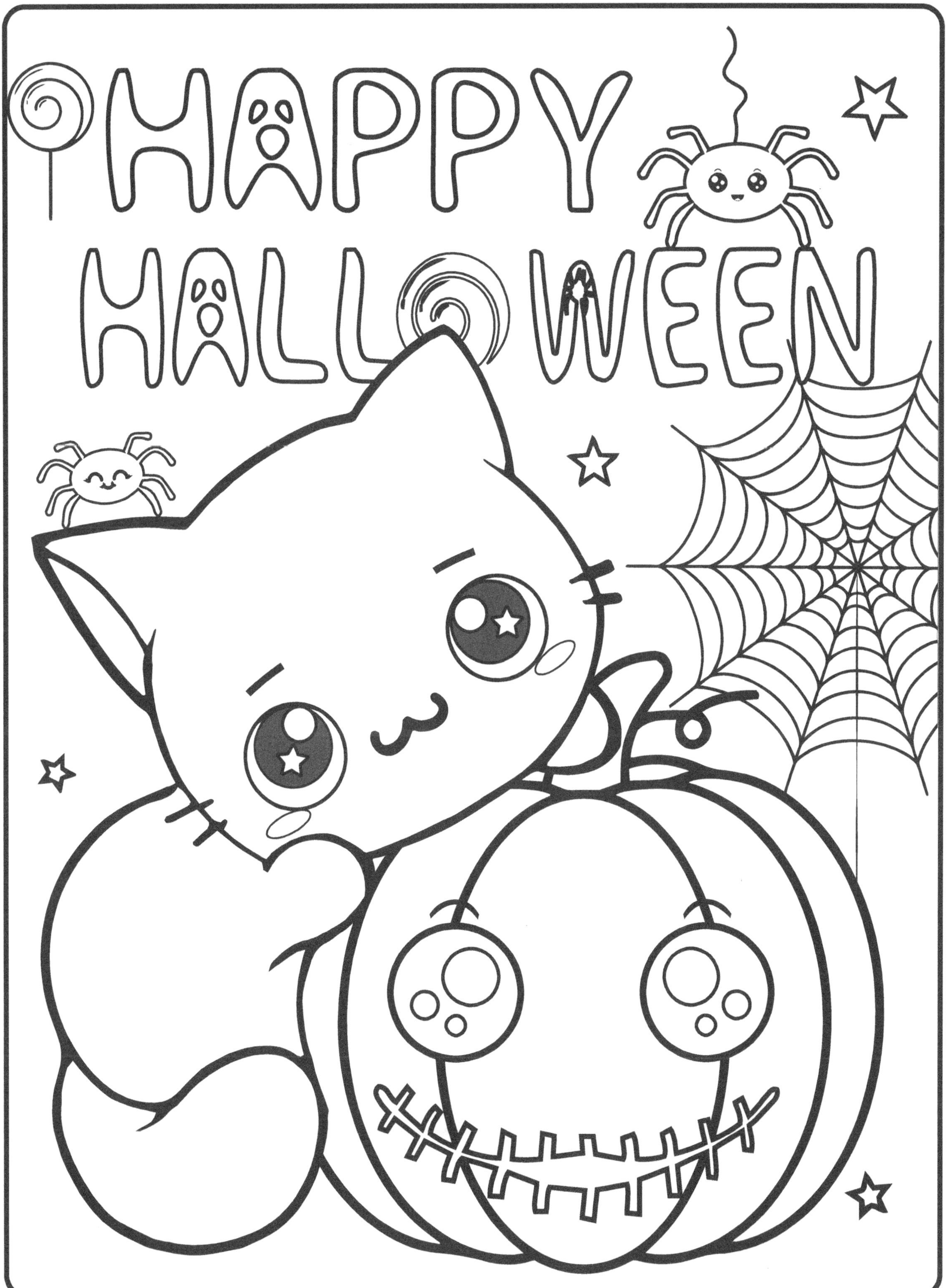
HAPPY
HALLOWEEN

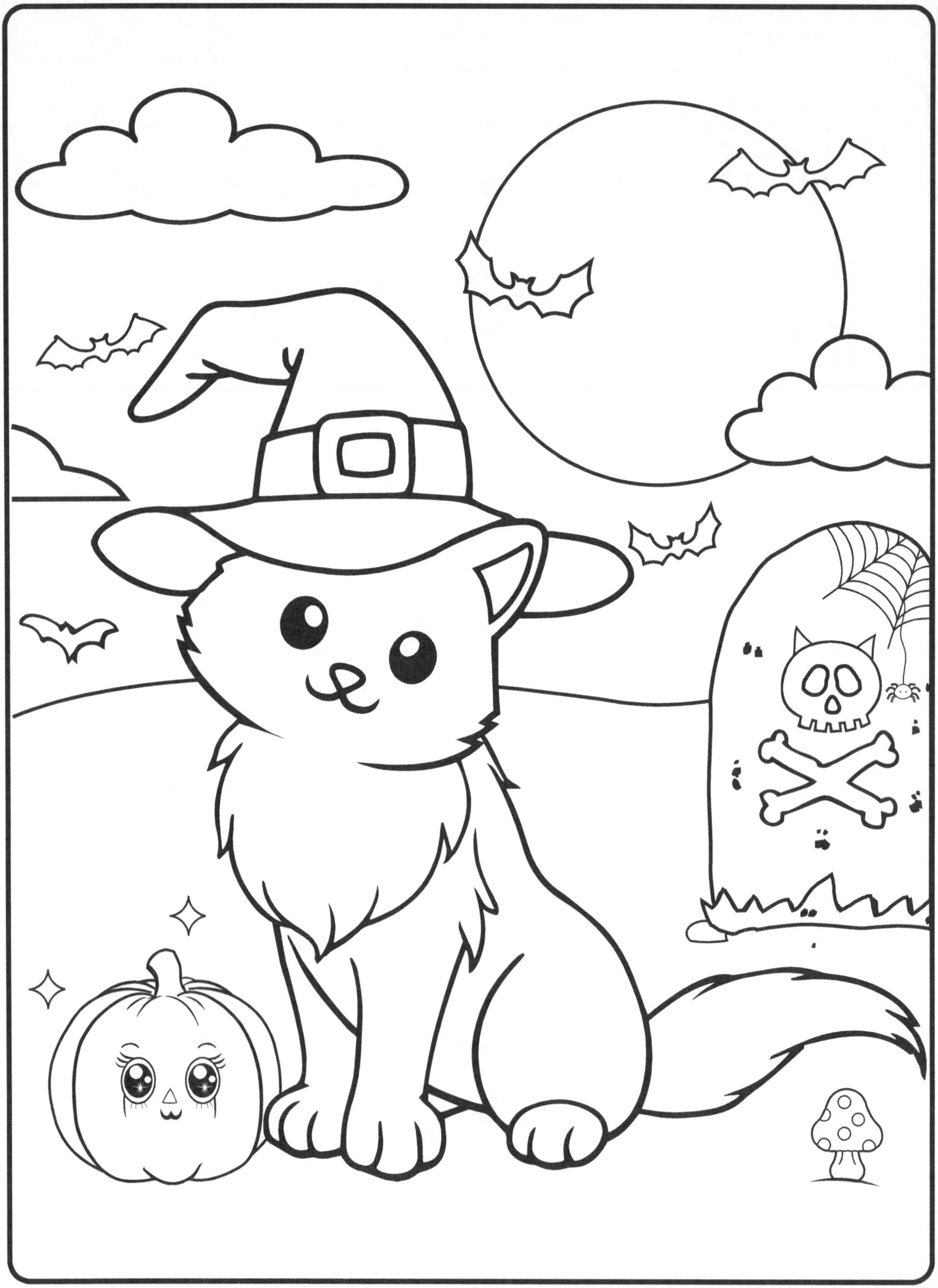

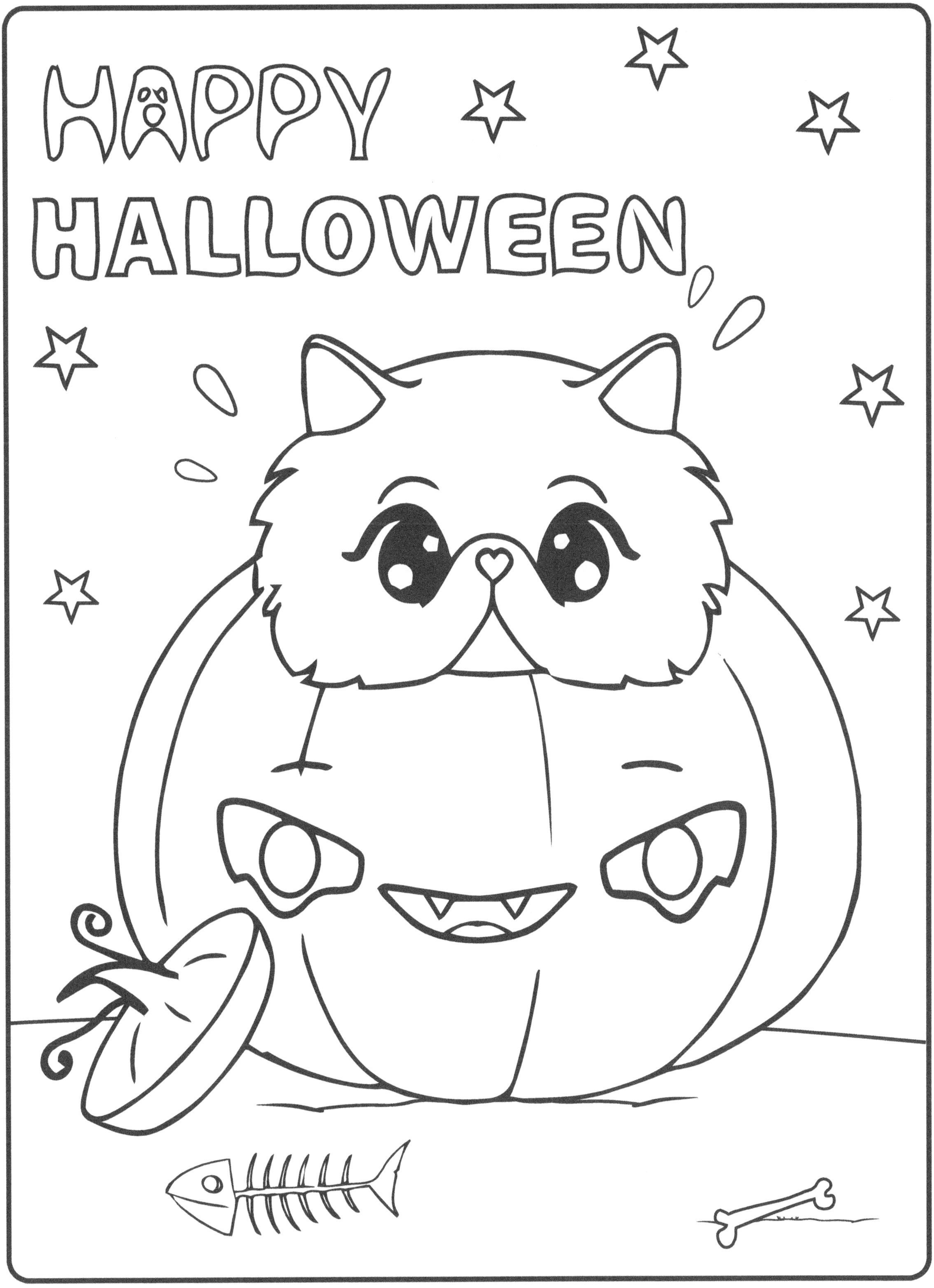
HAPPY
HALLOWEEN

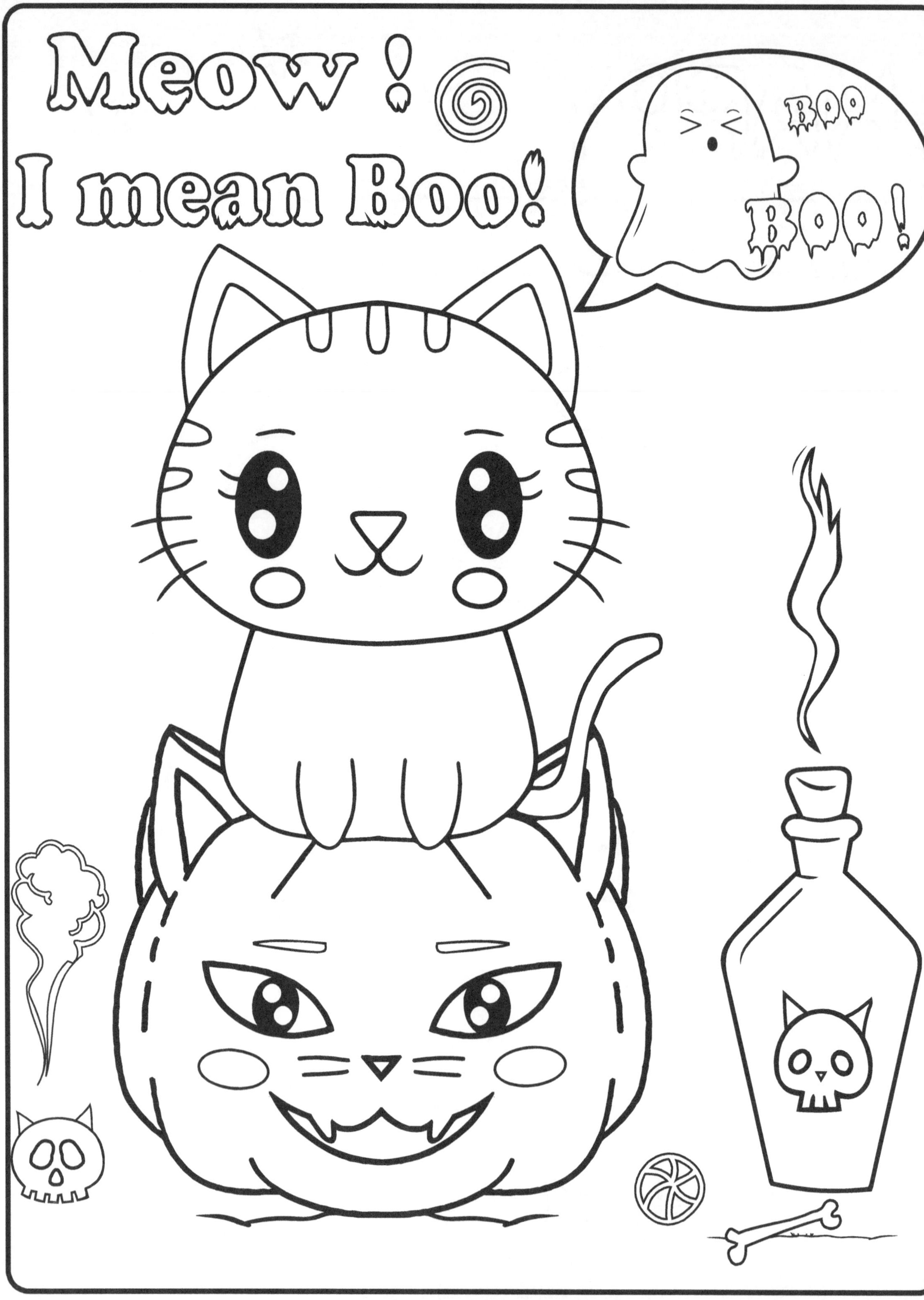
Meow !
I mean Boo!
BOO
BOO!

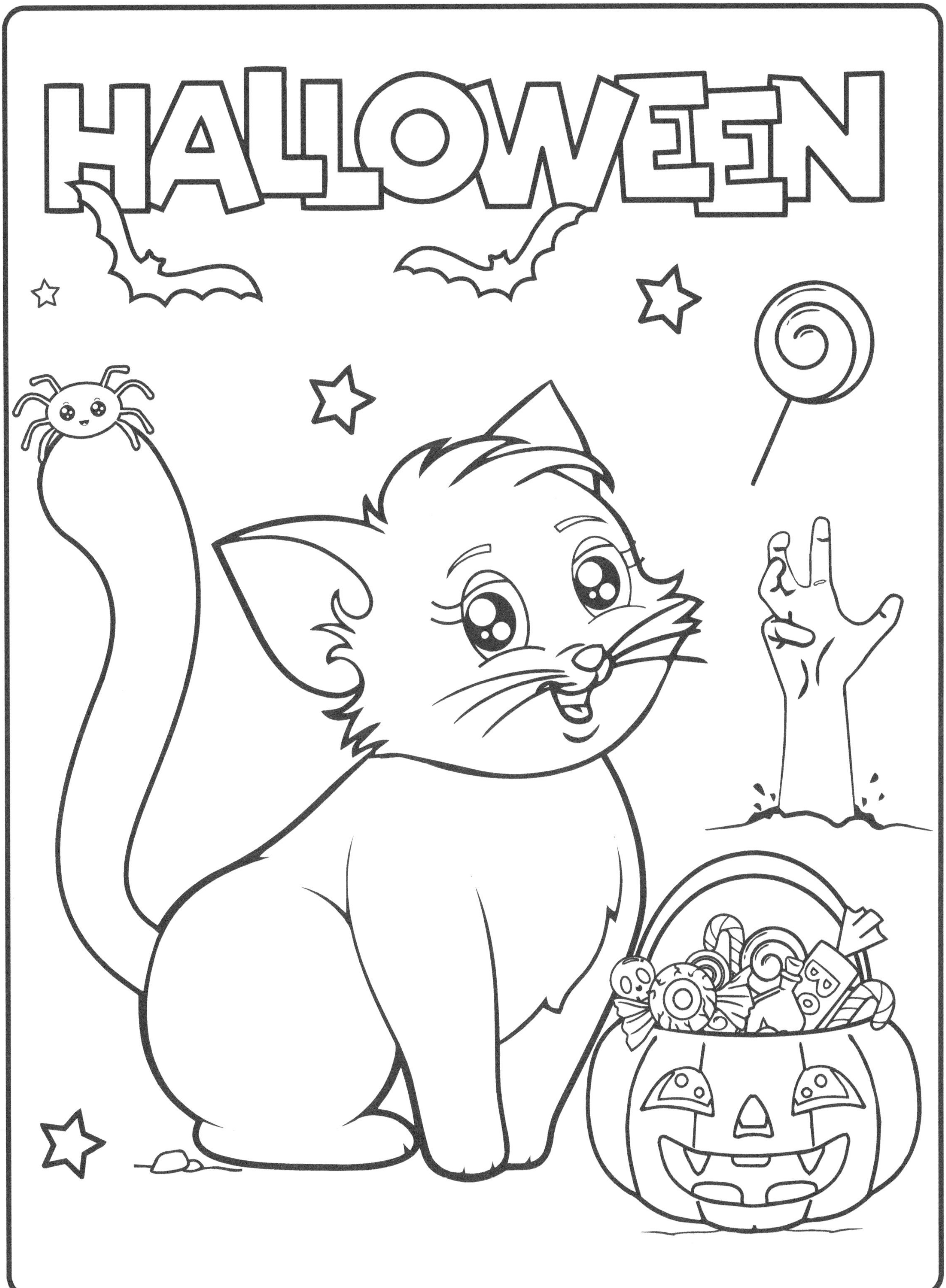
HALLOWEEN

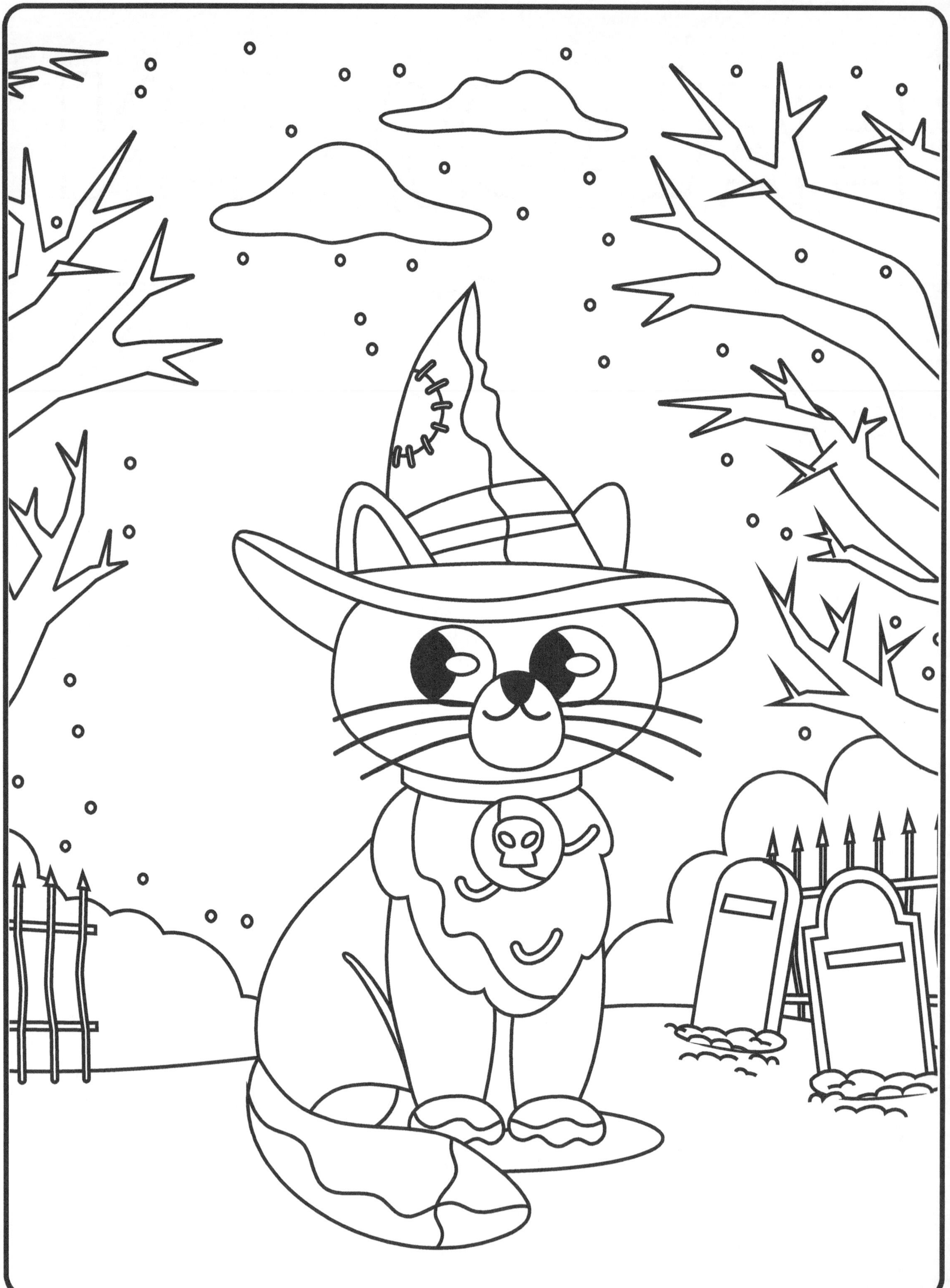

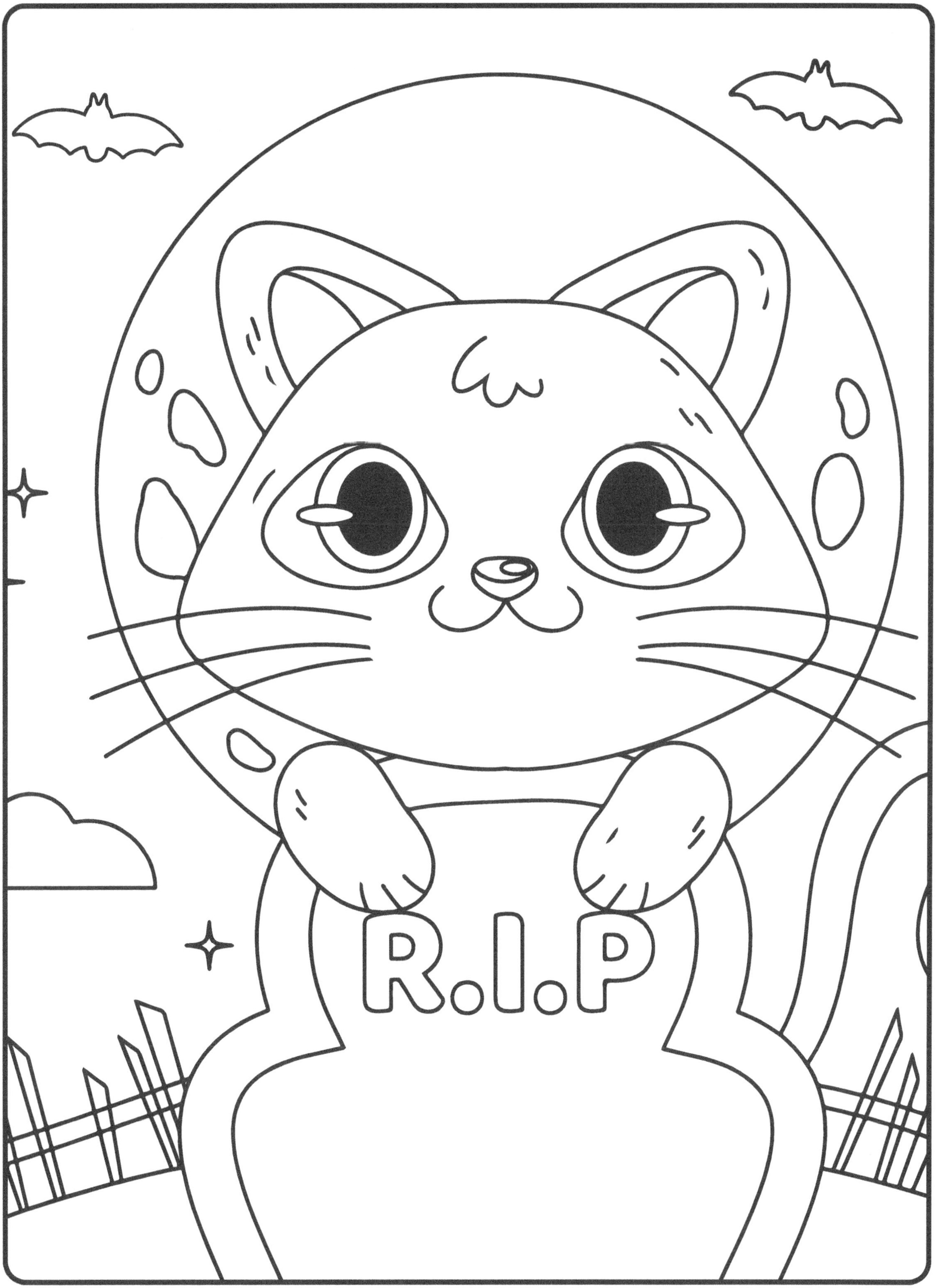
R.I.P

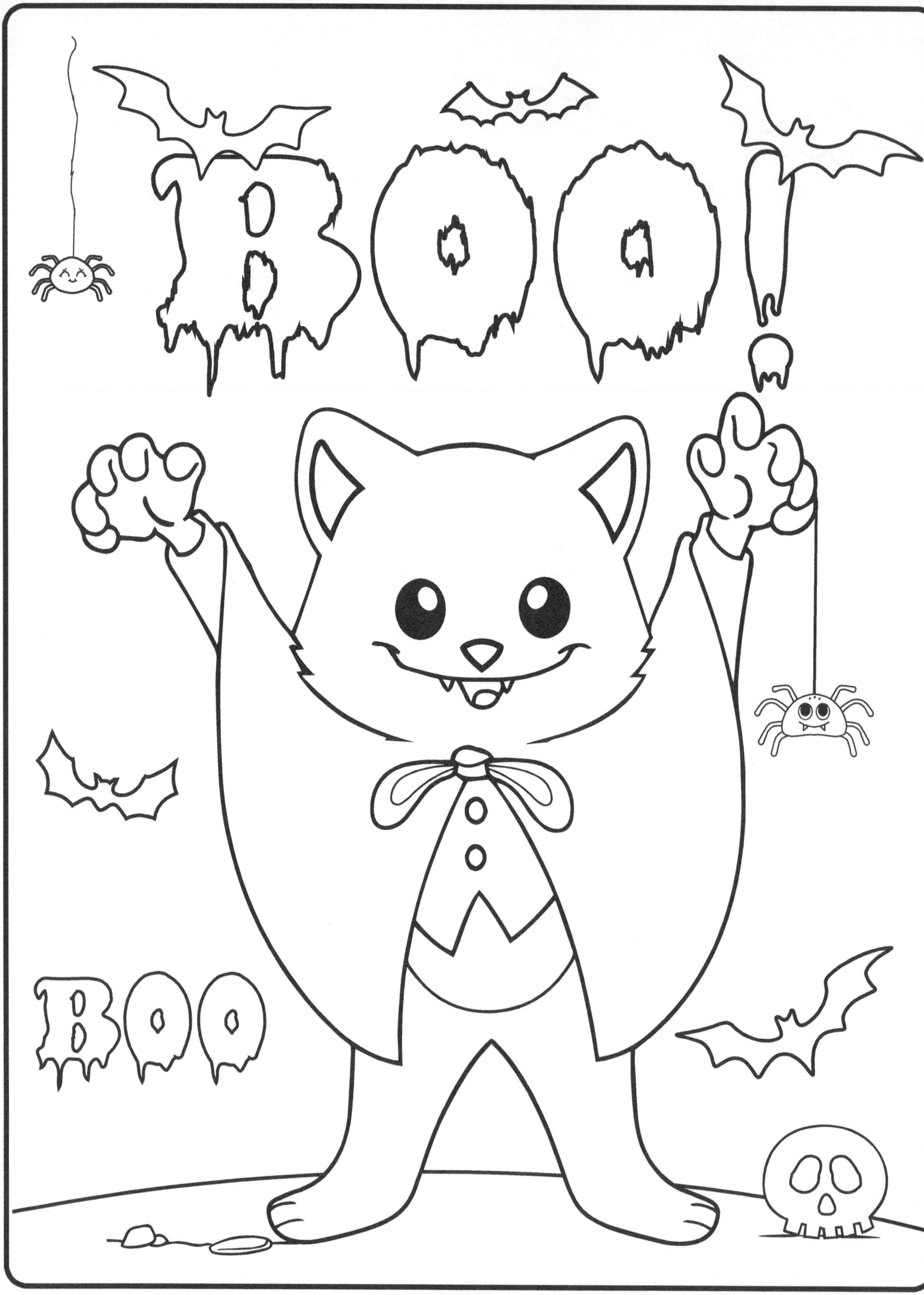
BOO!
BOO

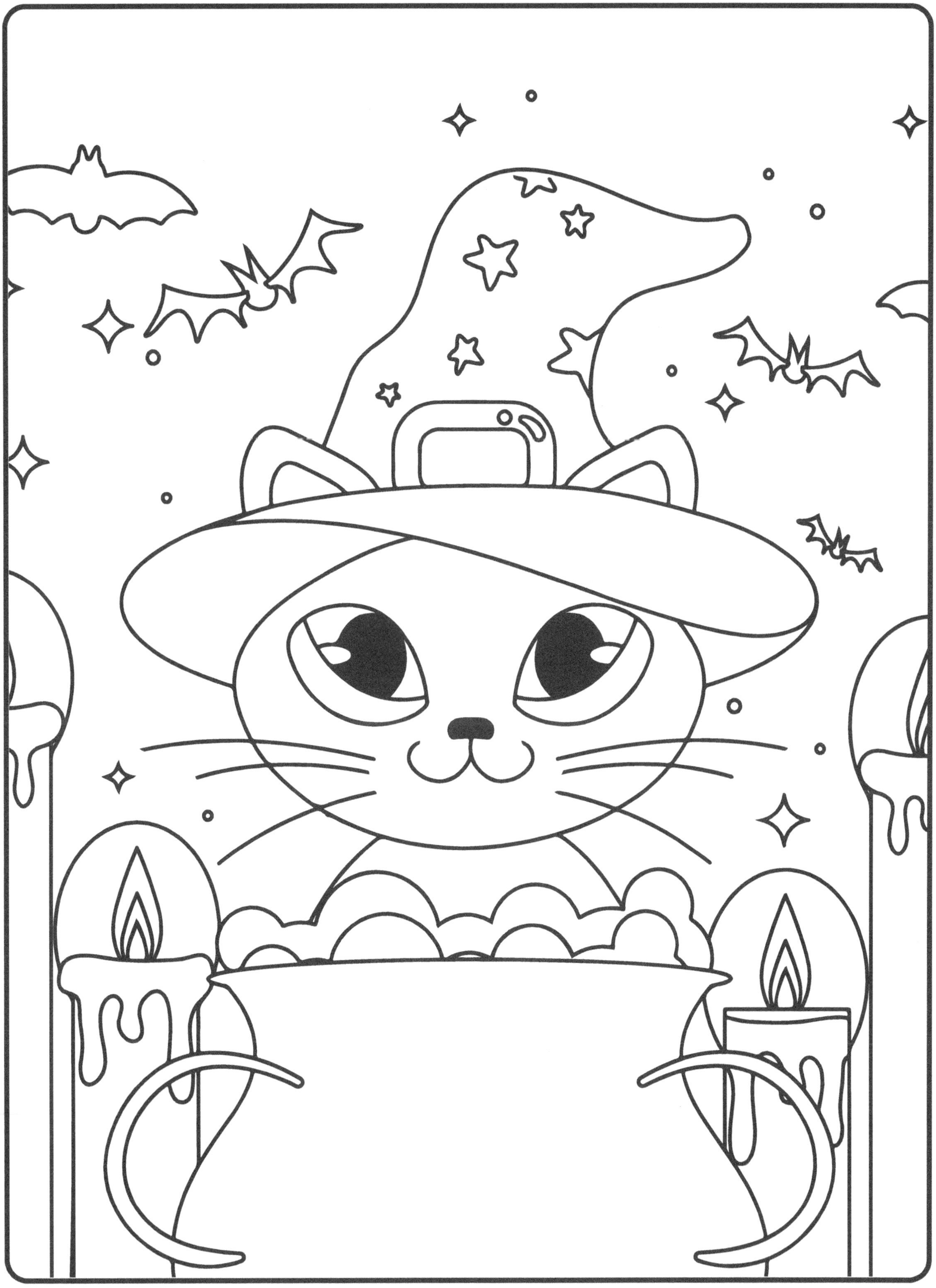

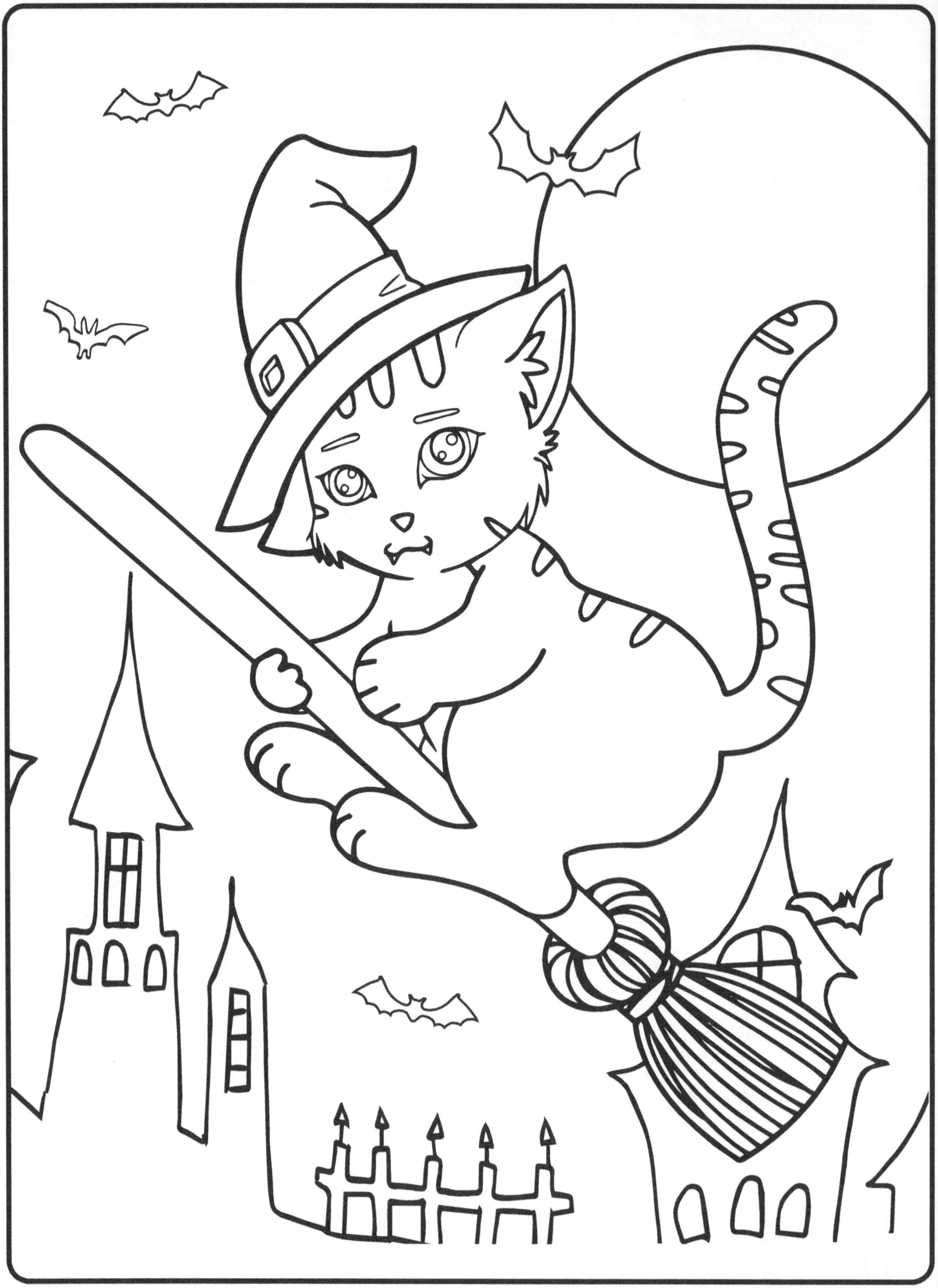

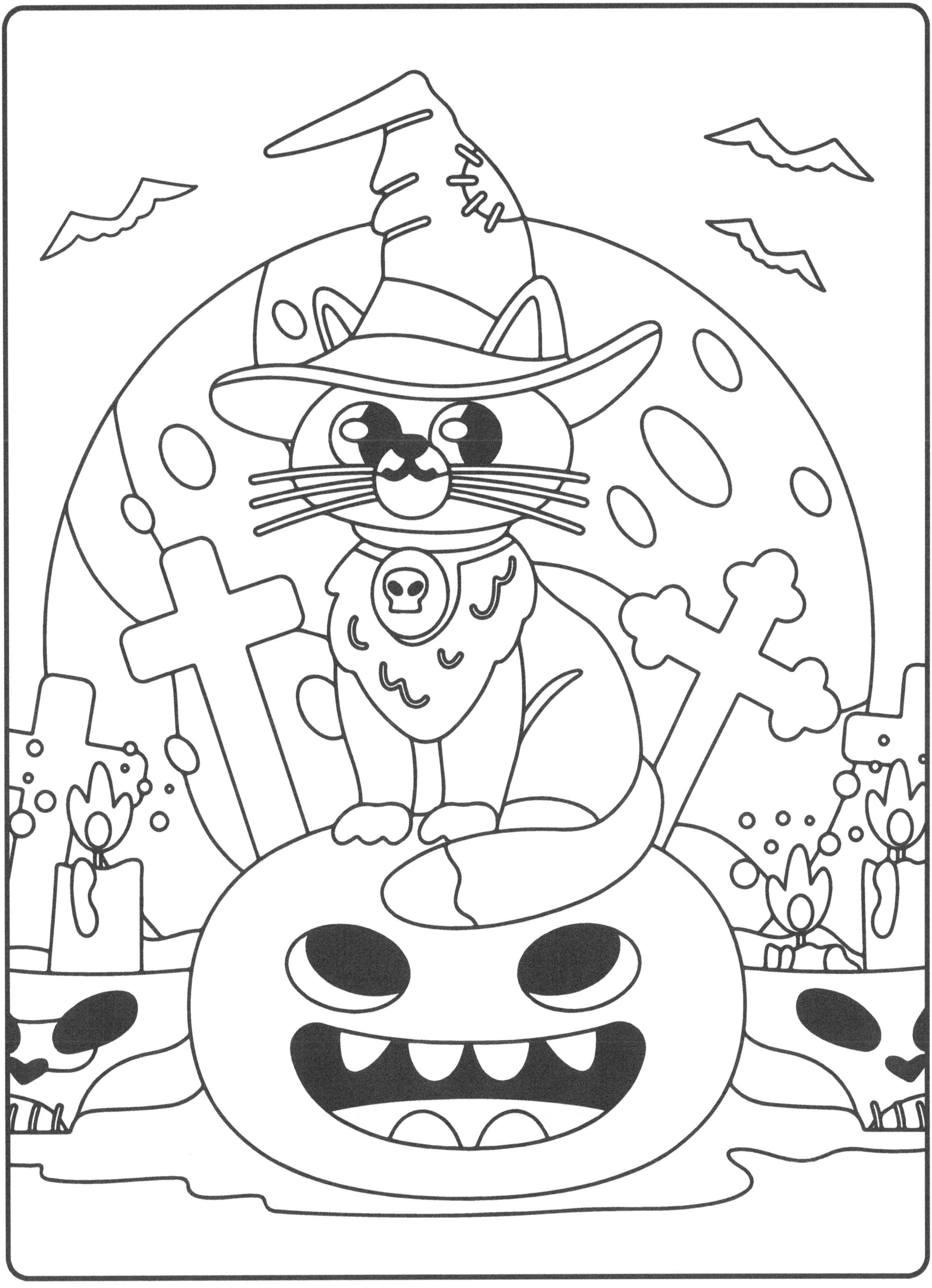

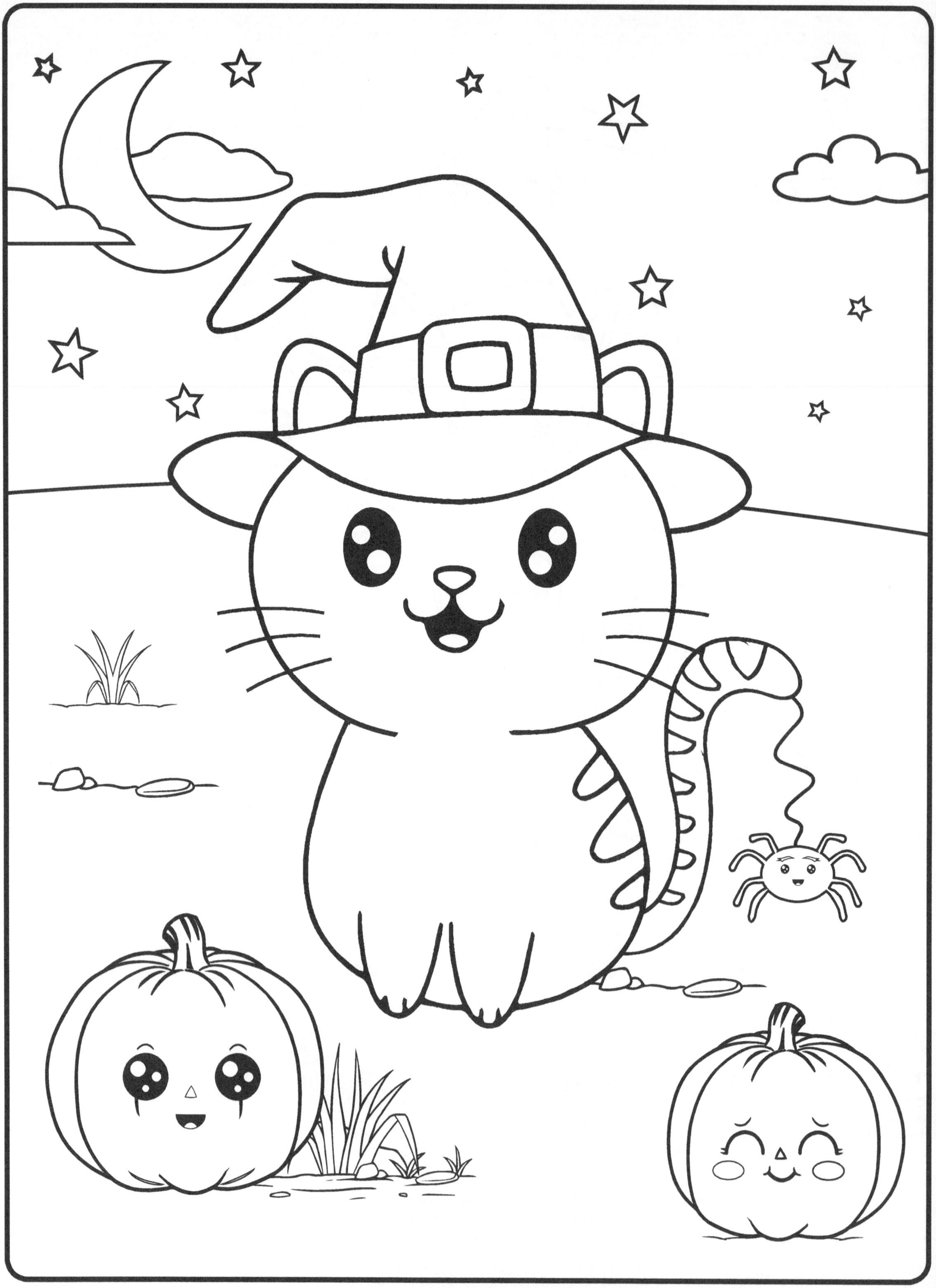

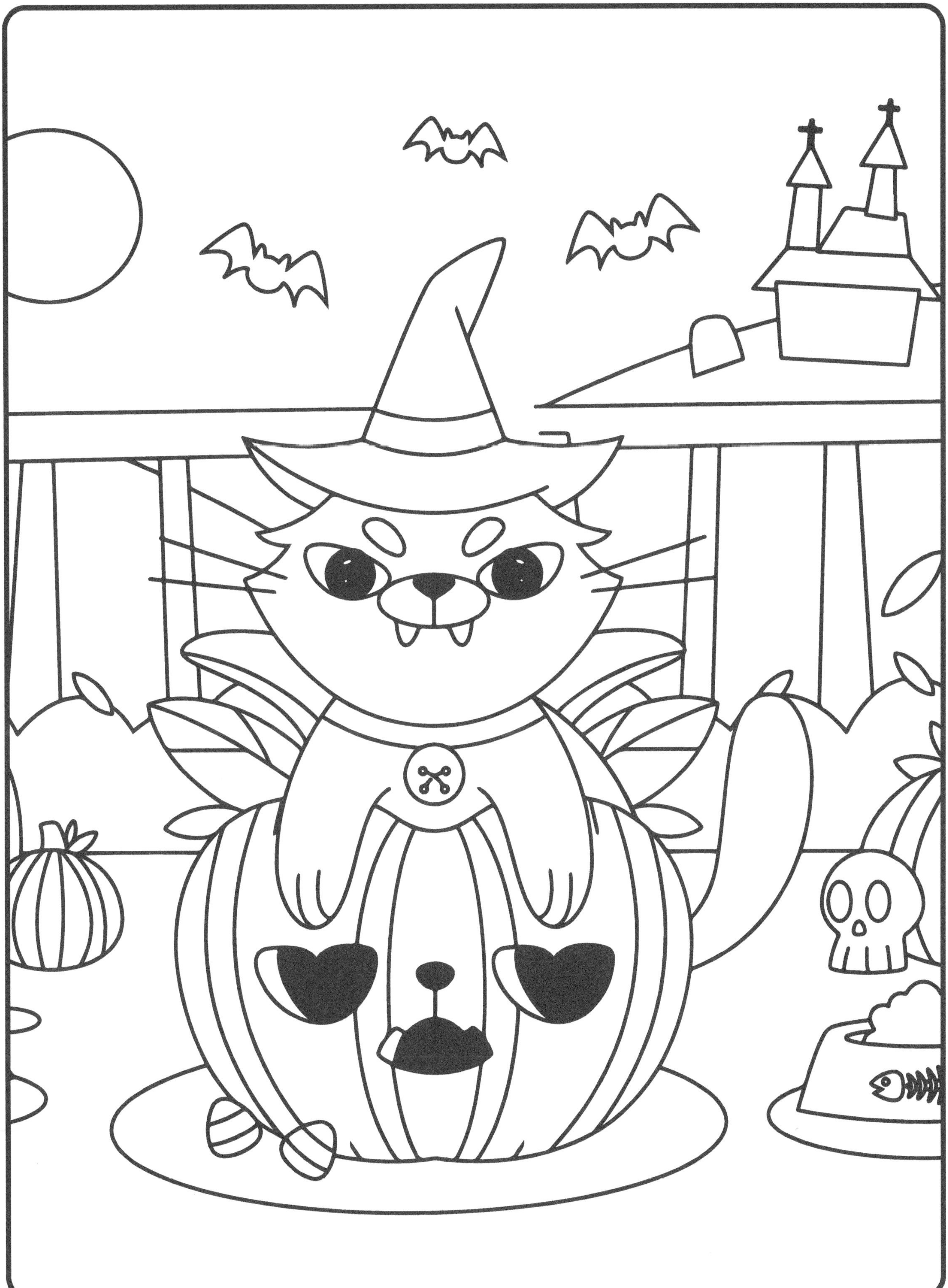

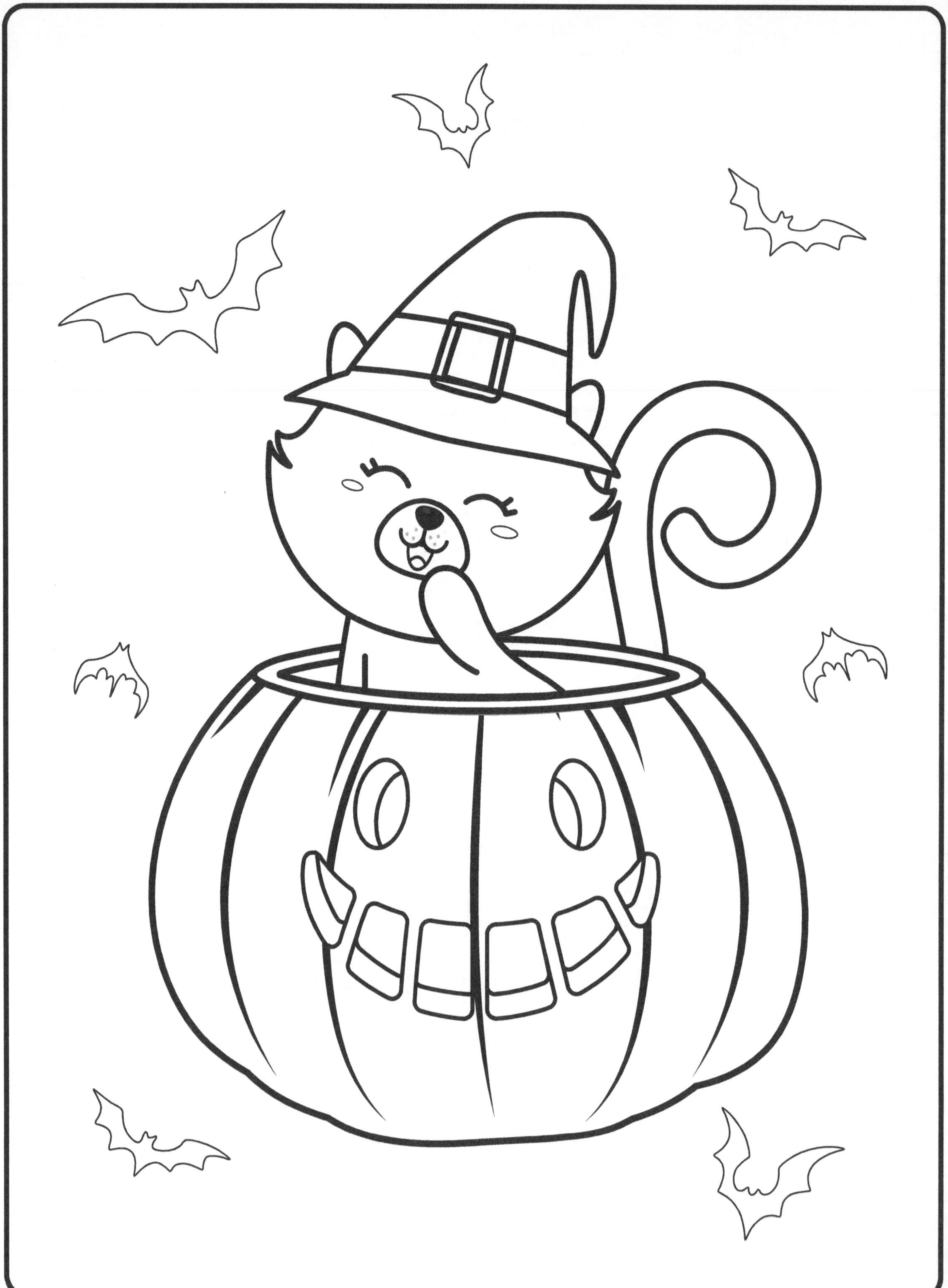

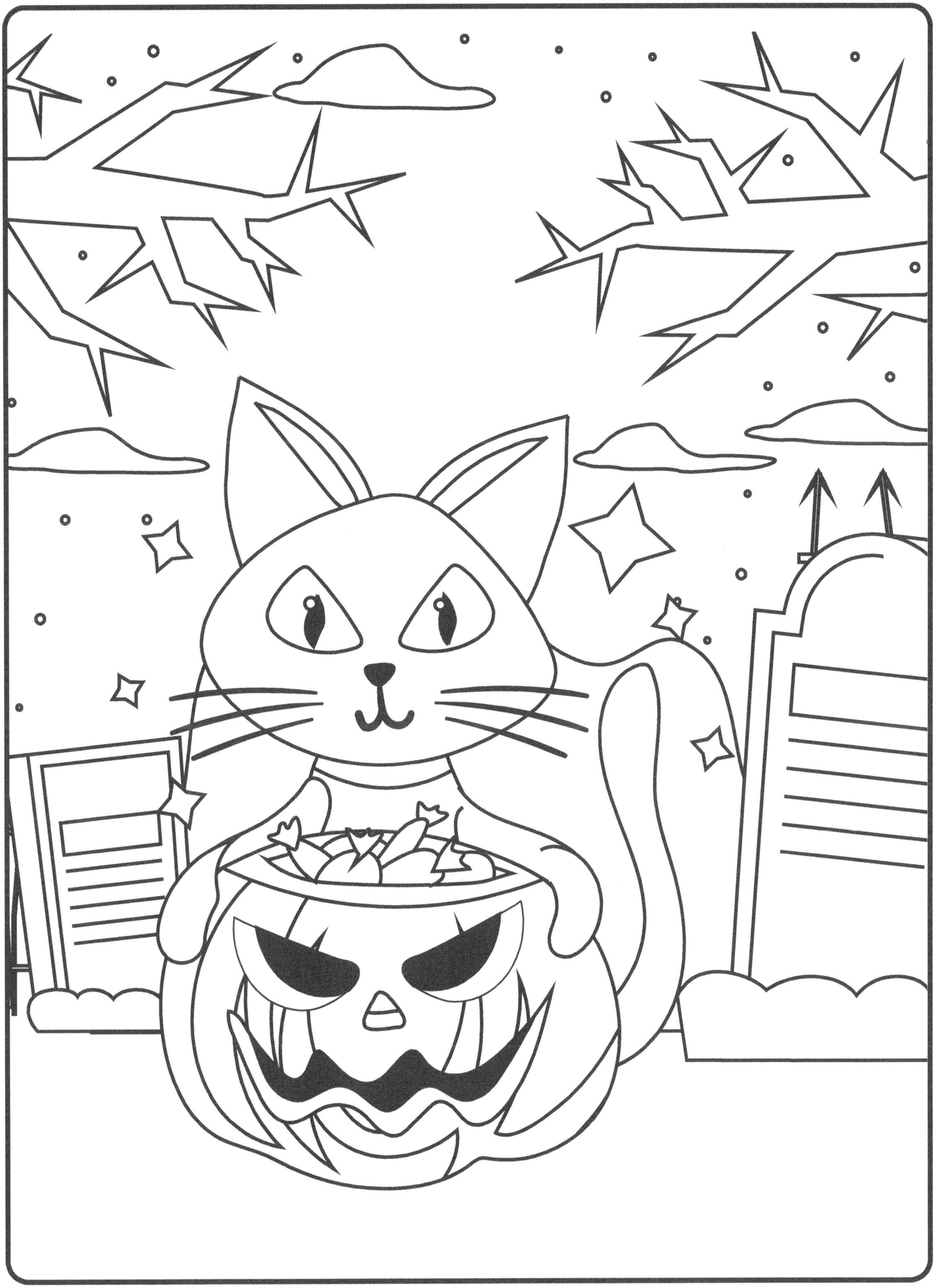

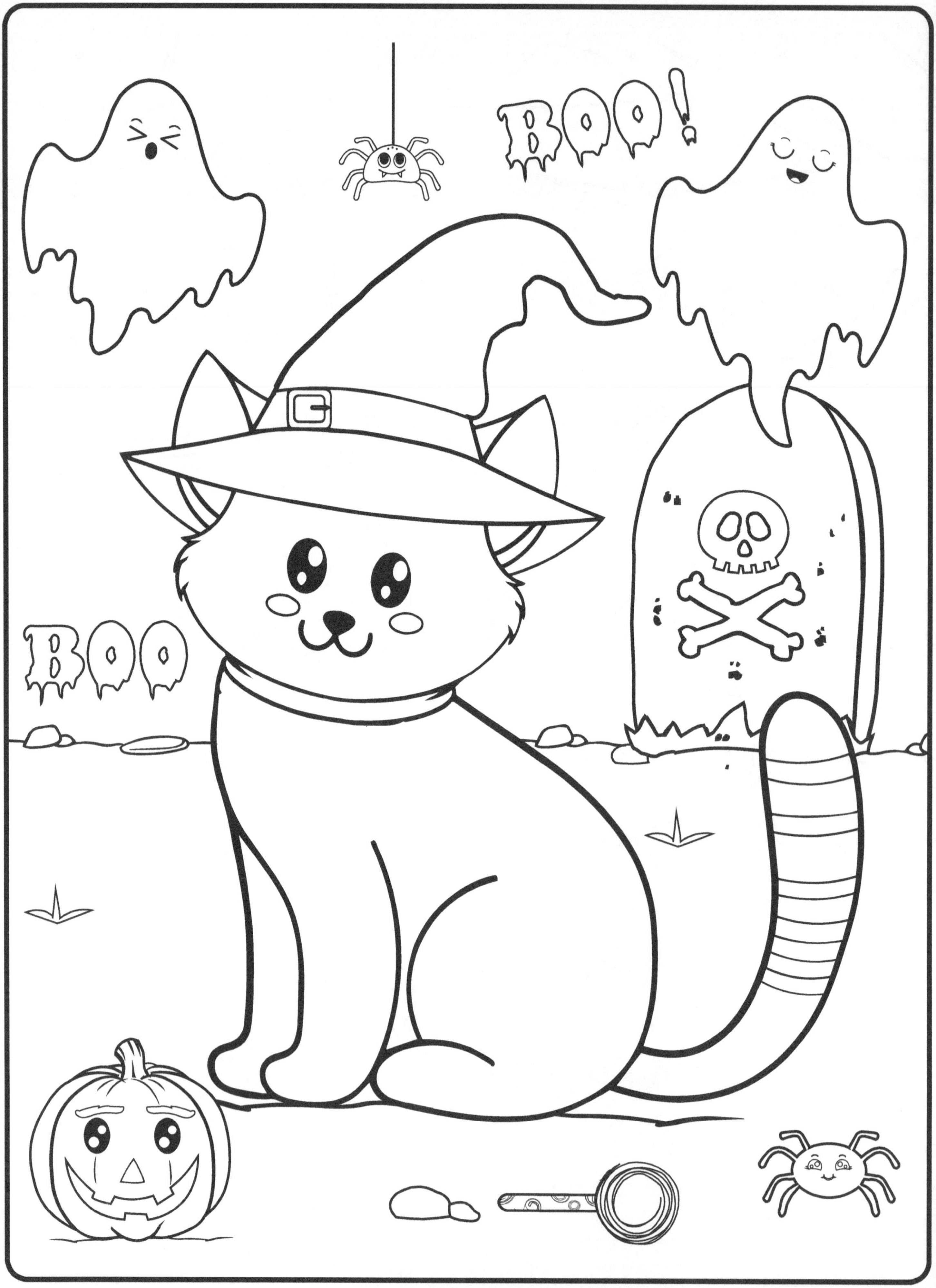
BOO!
BOO

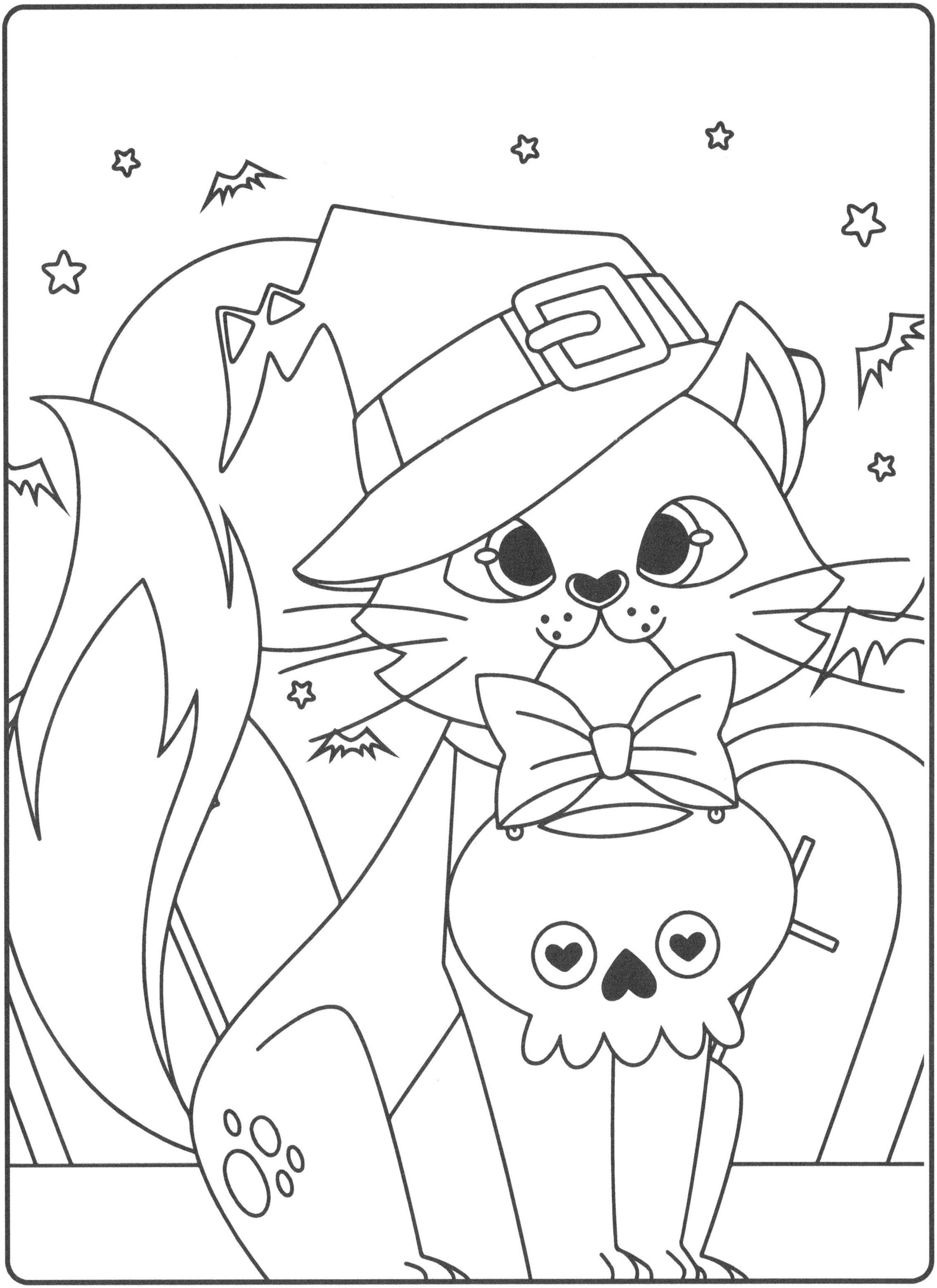

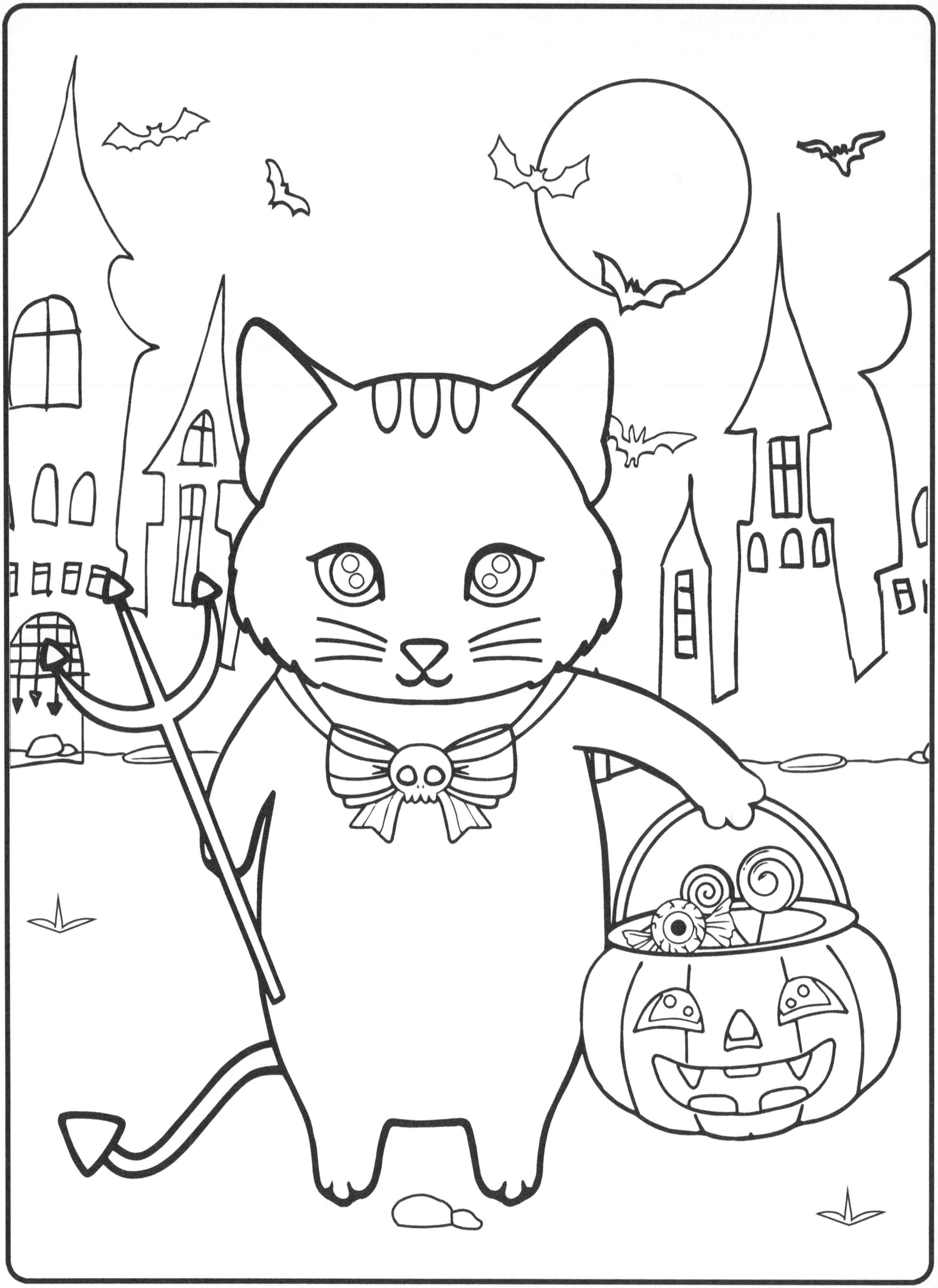

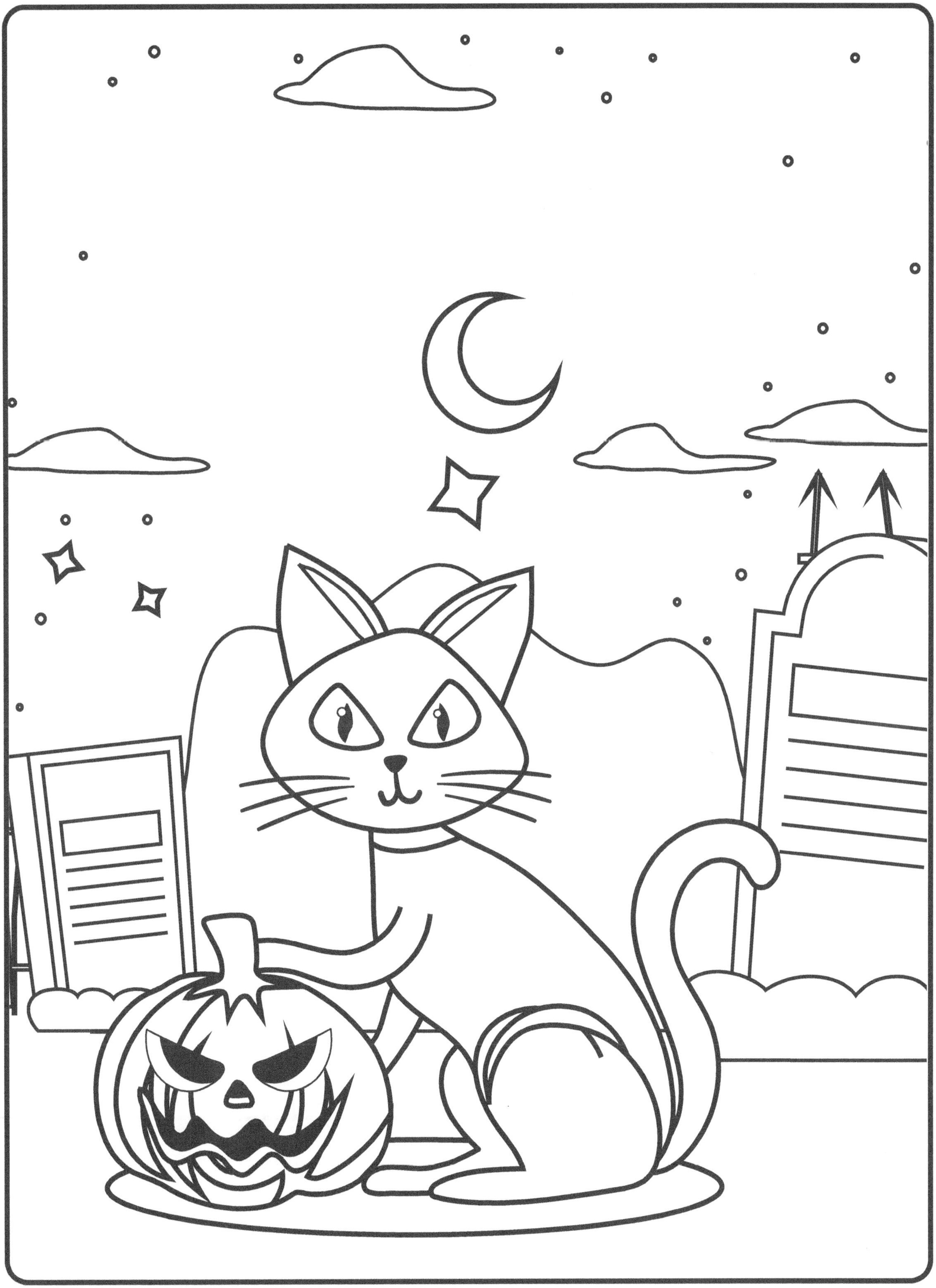

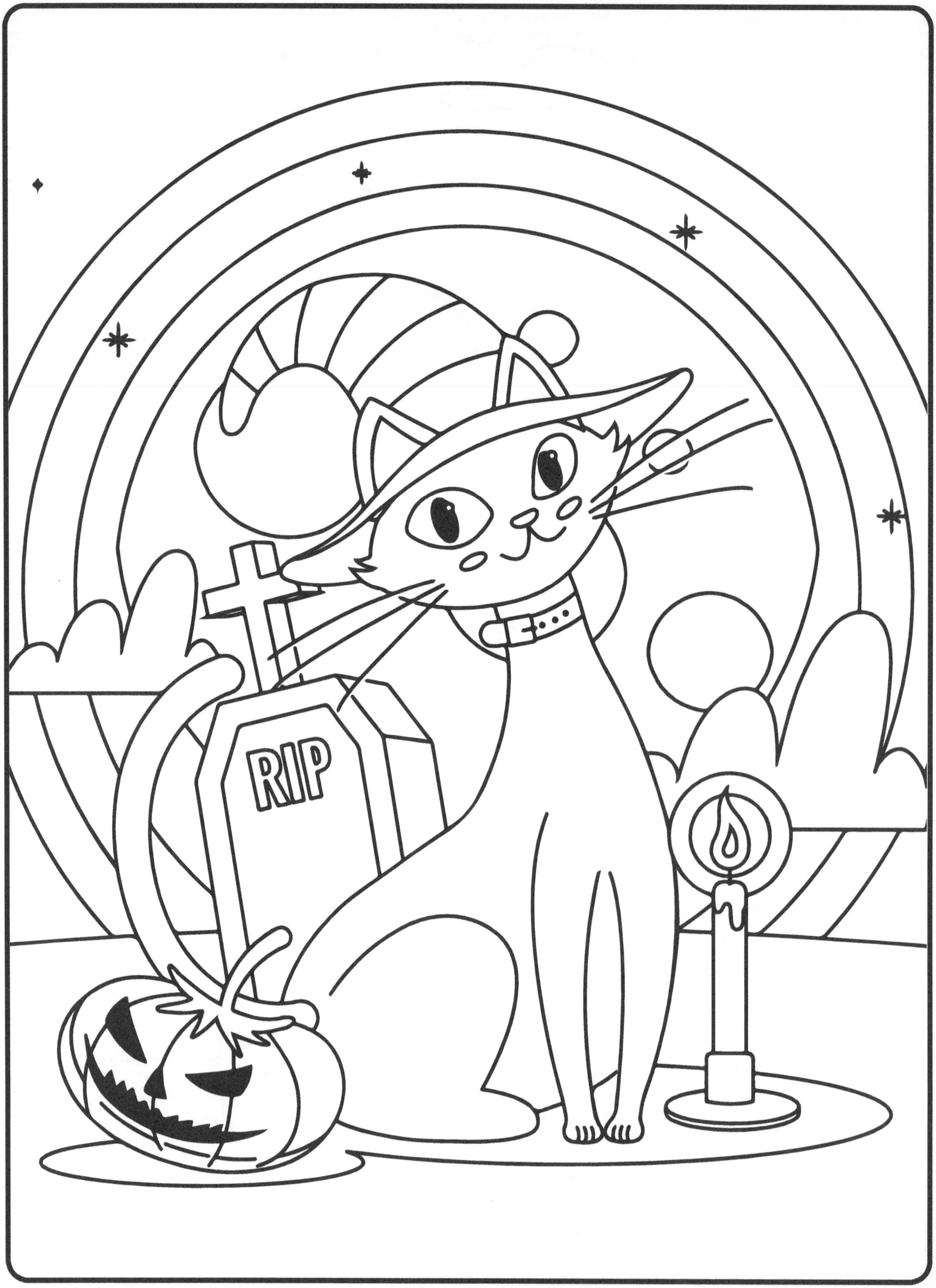
RIP

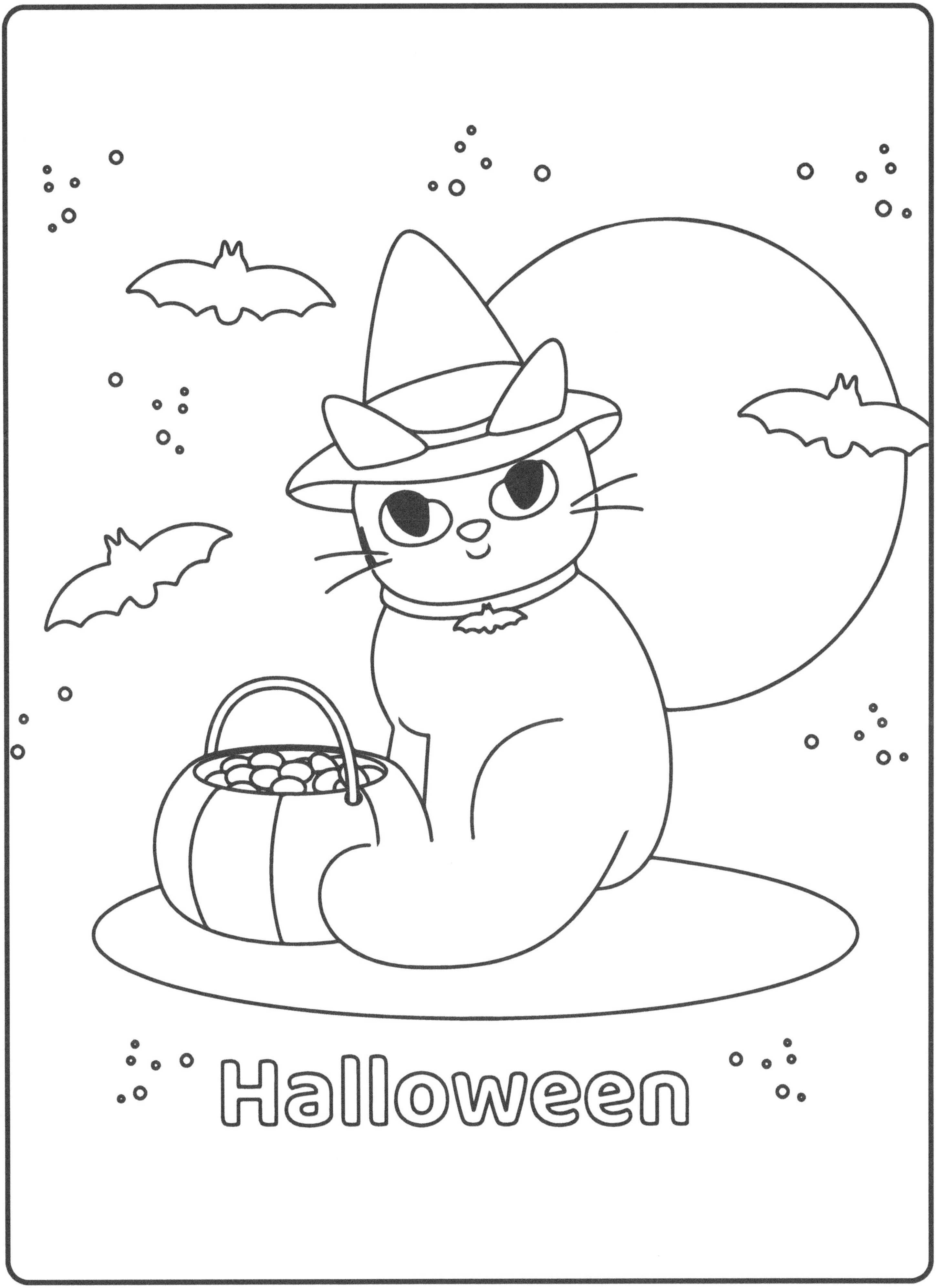
Halloween

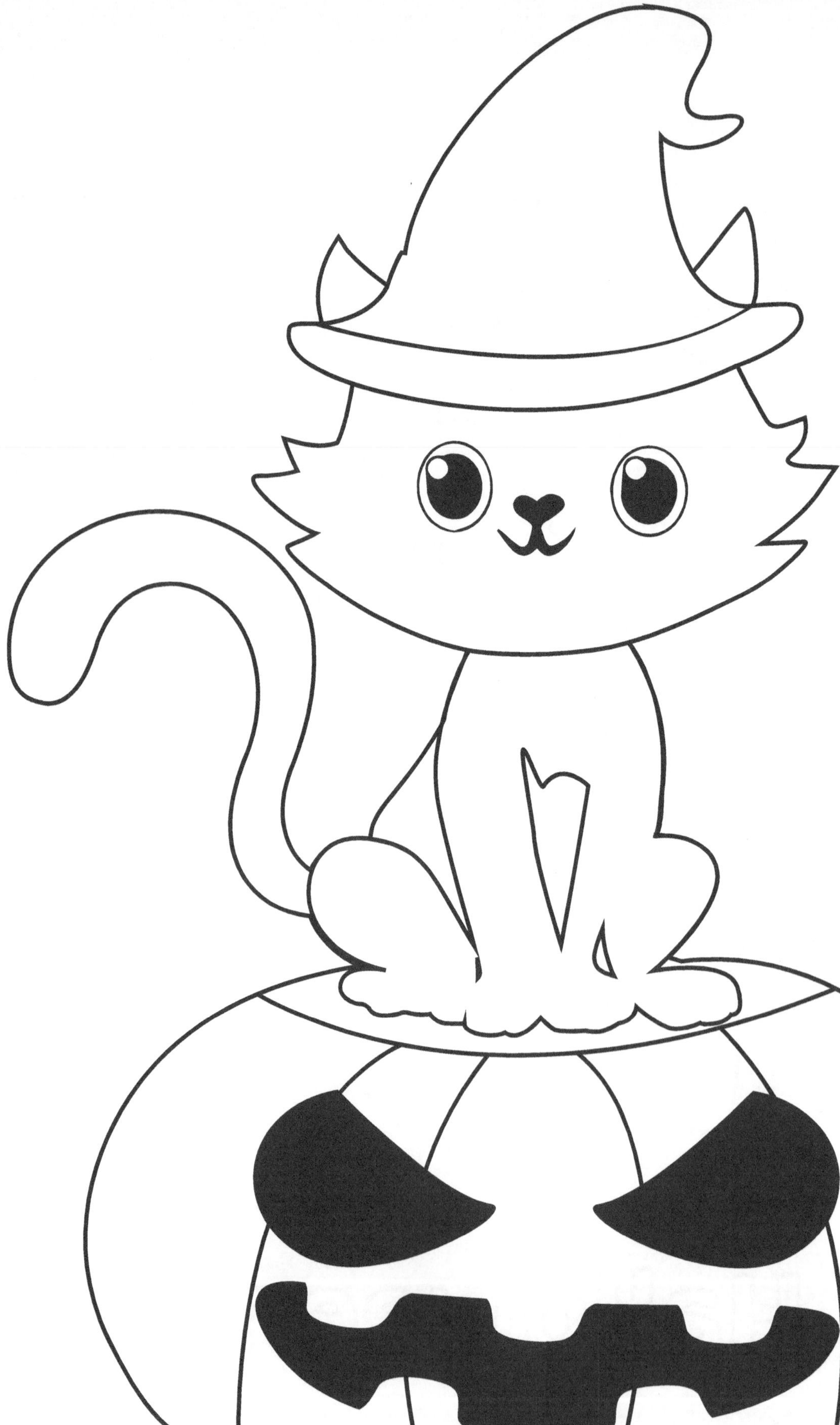

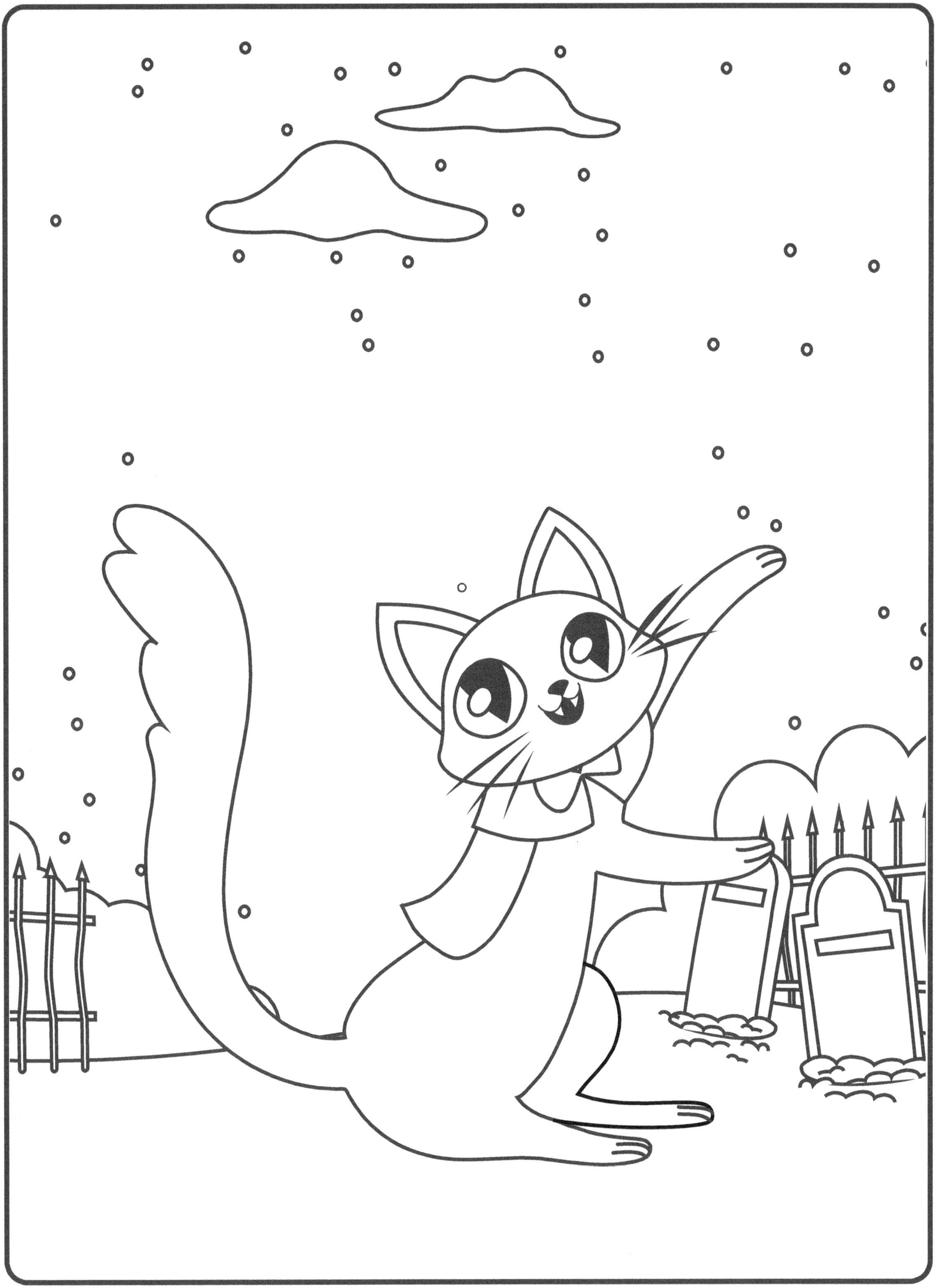

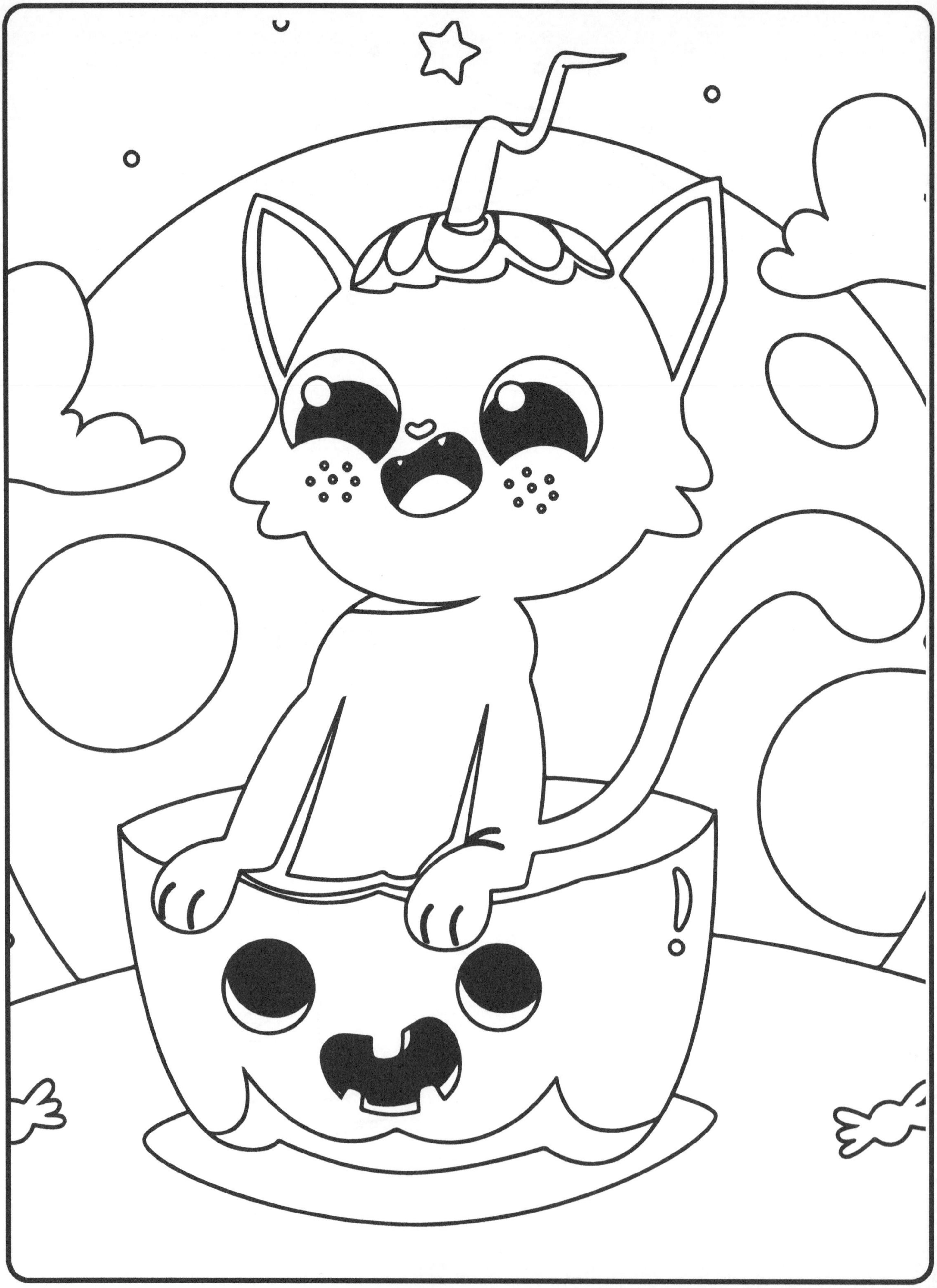

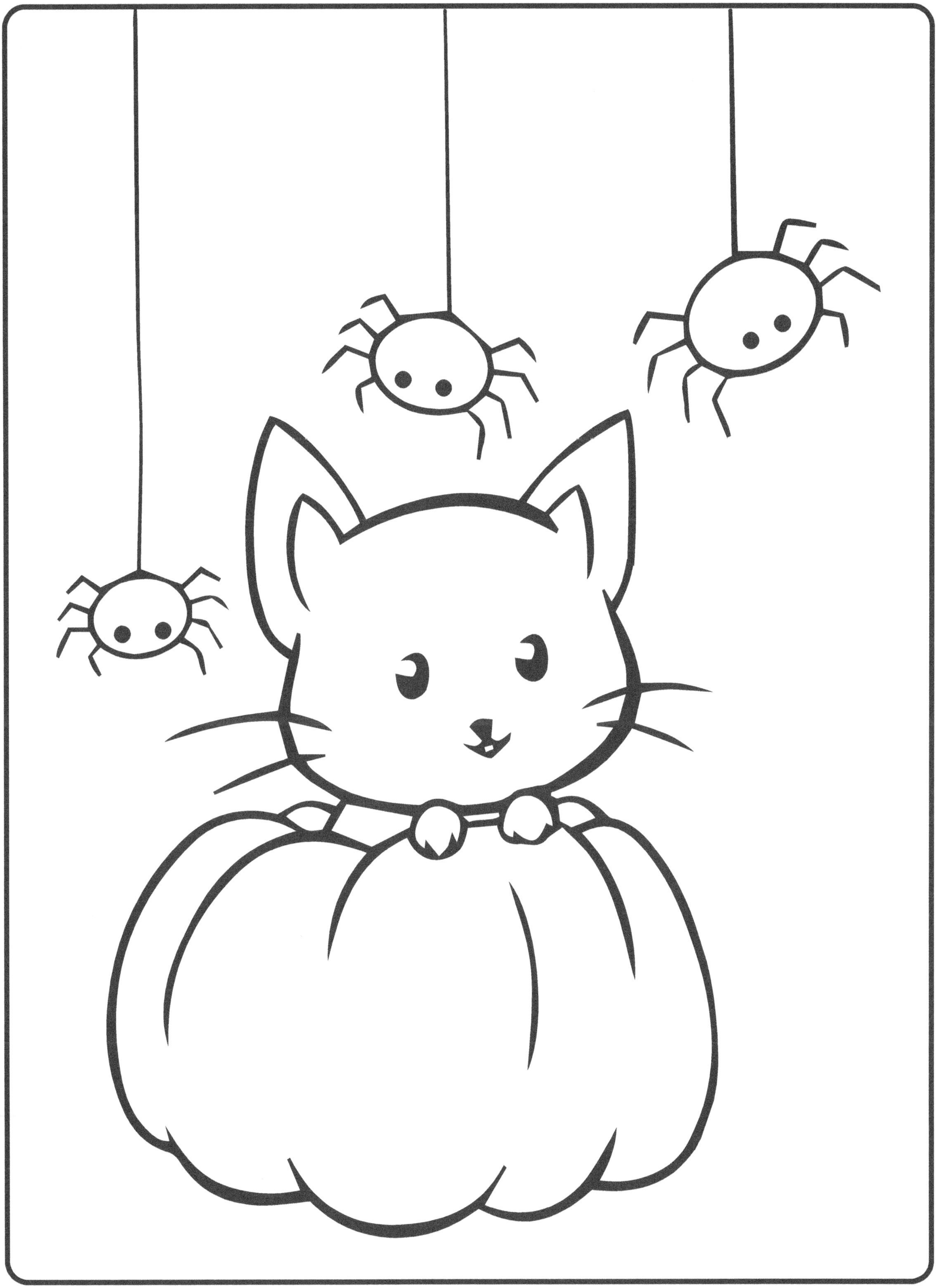

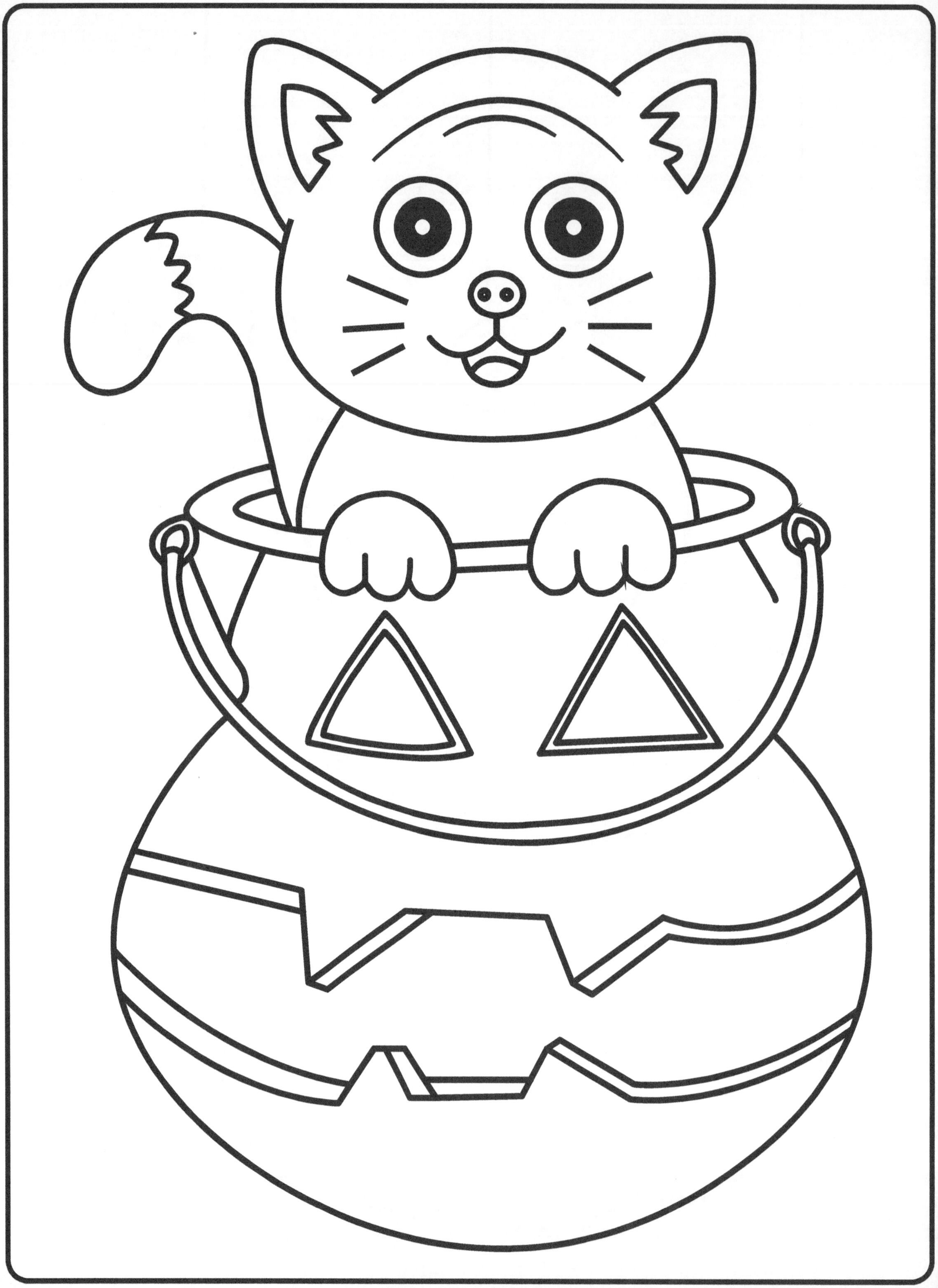

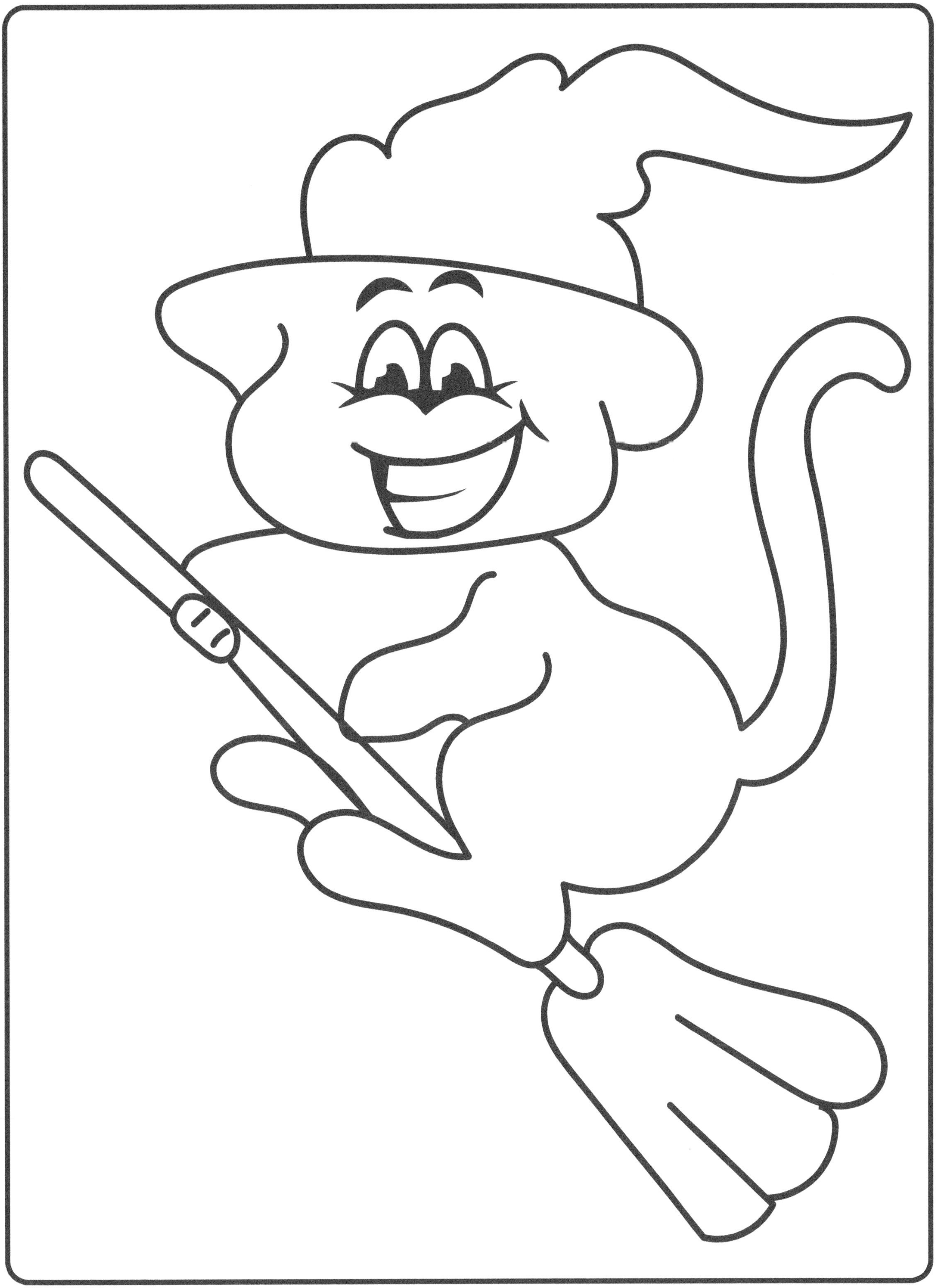

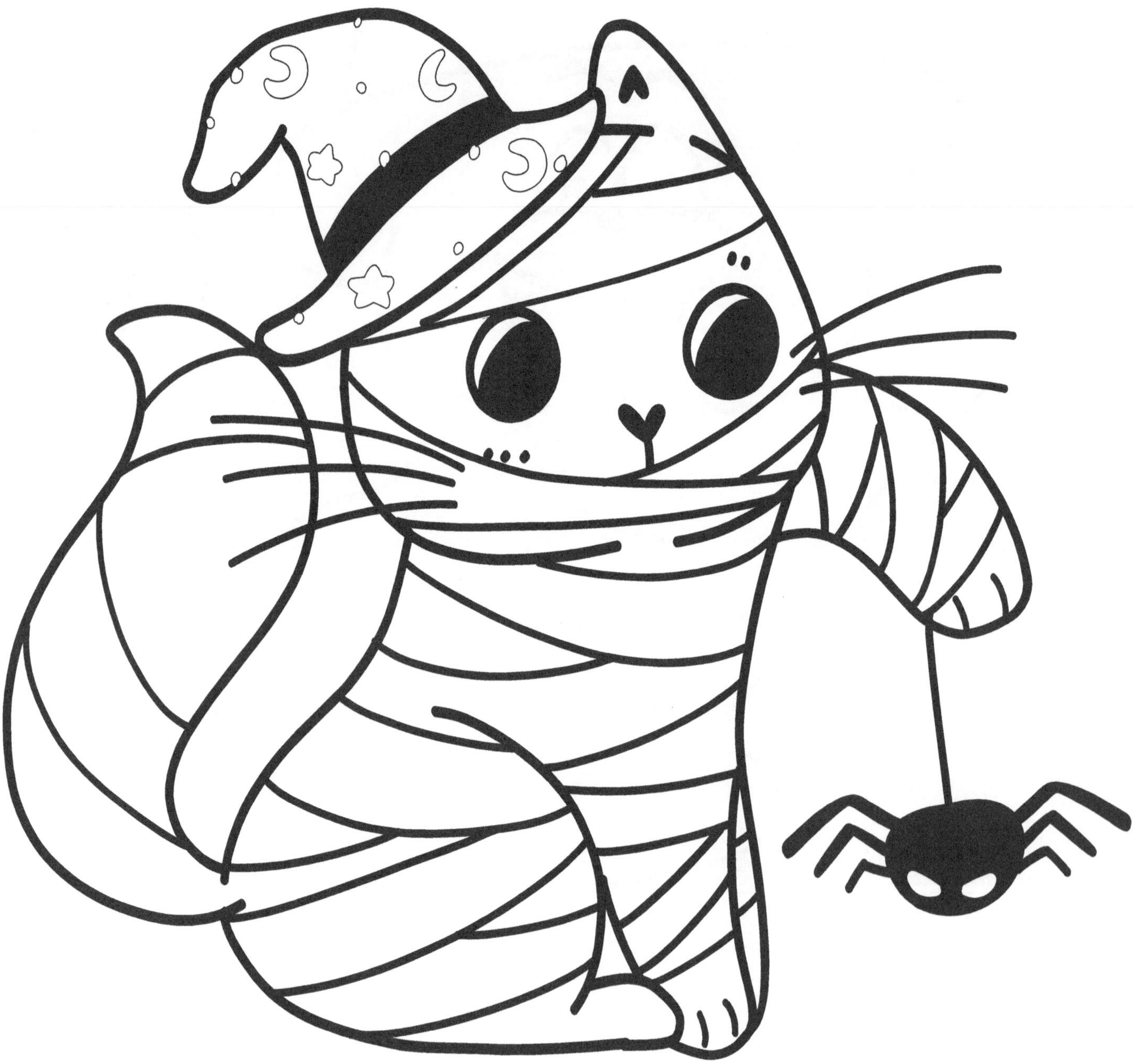

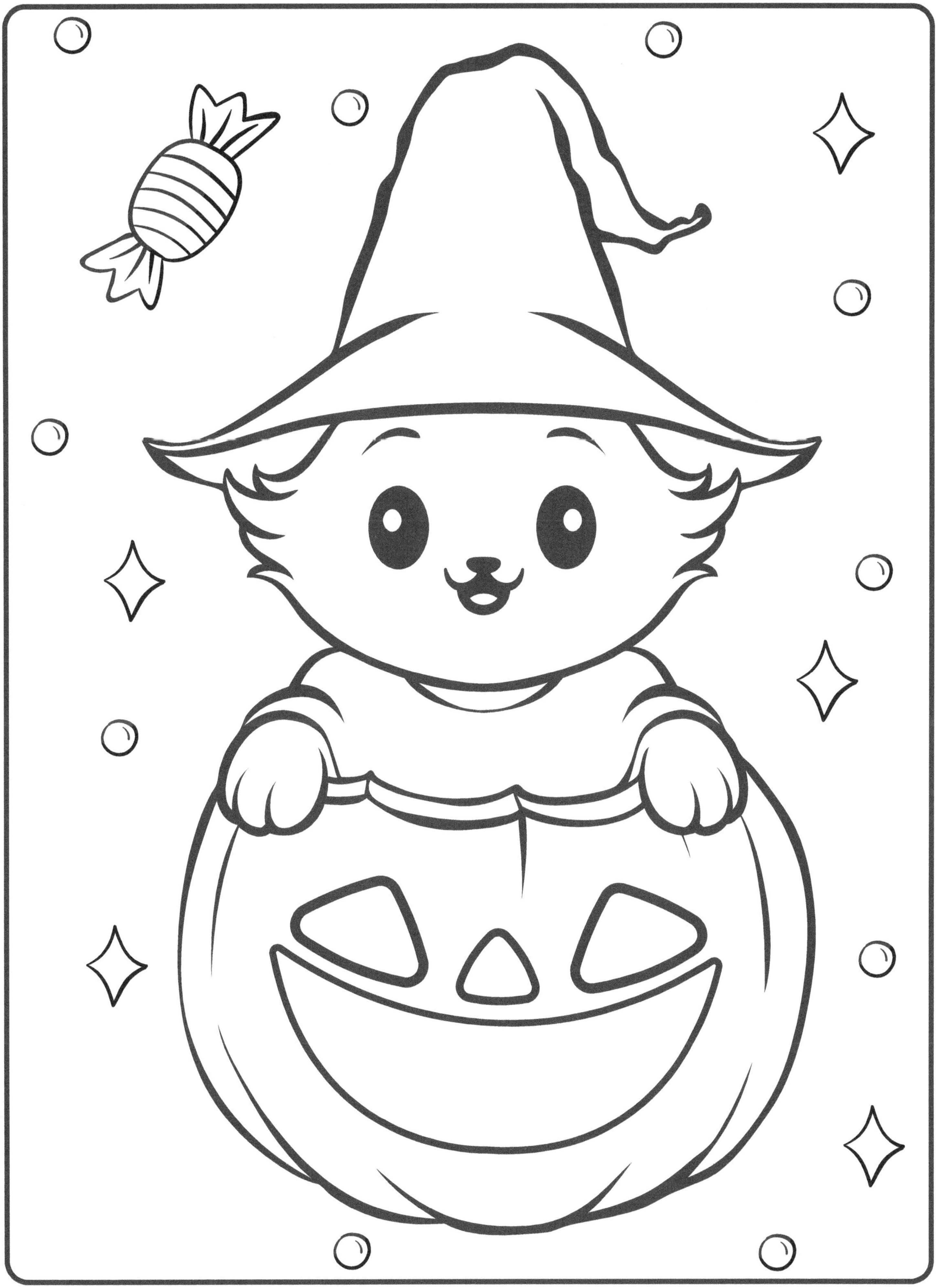

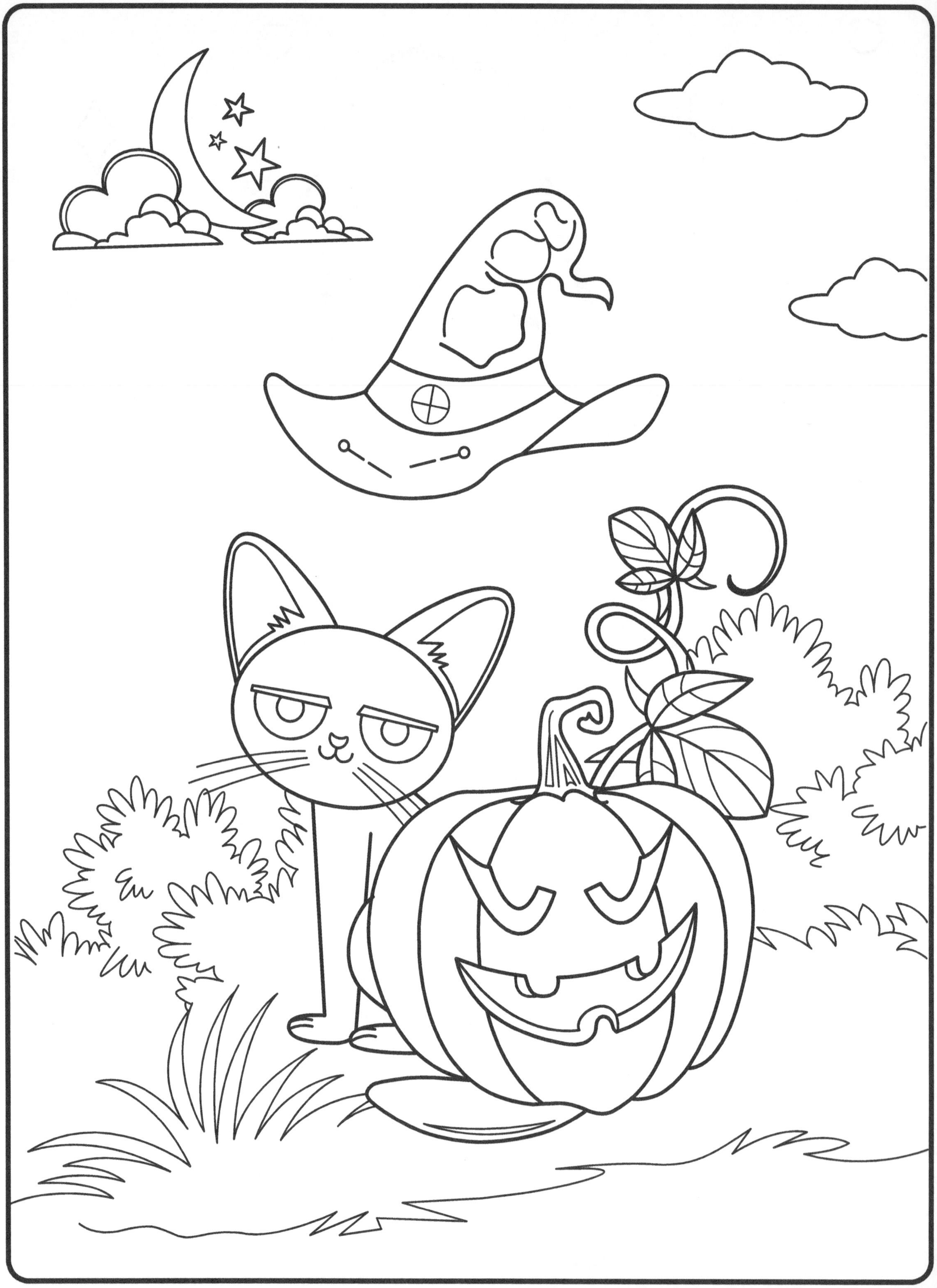

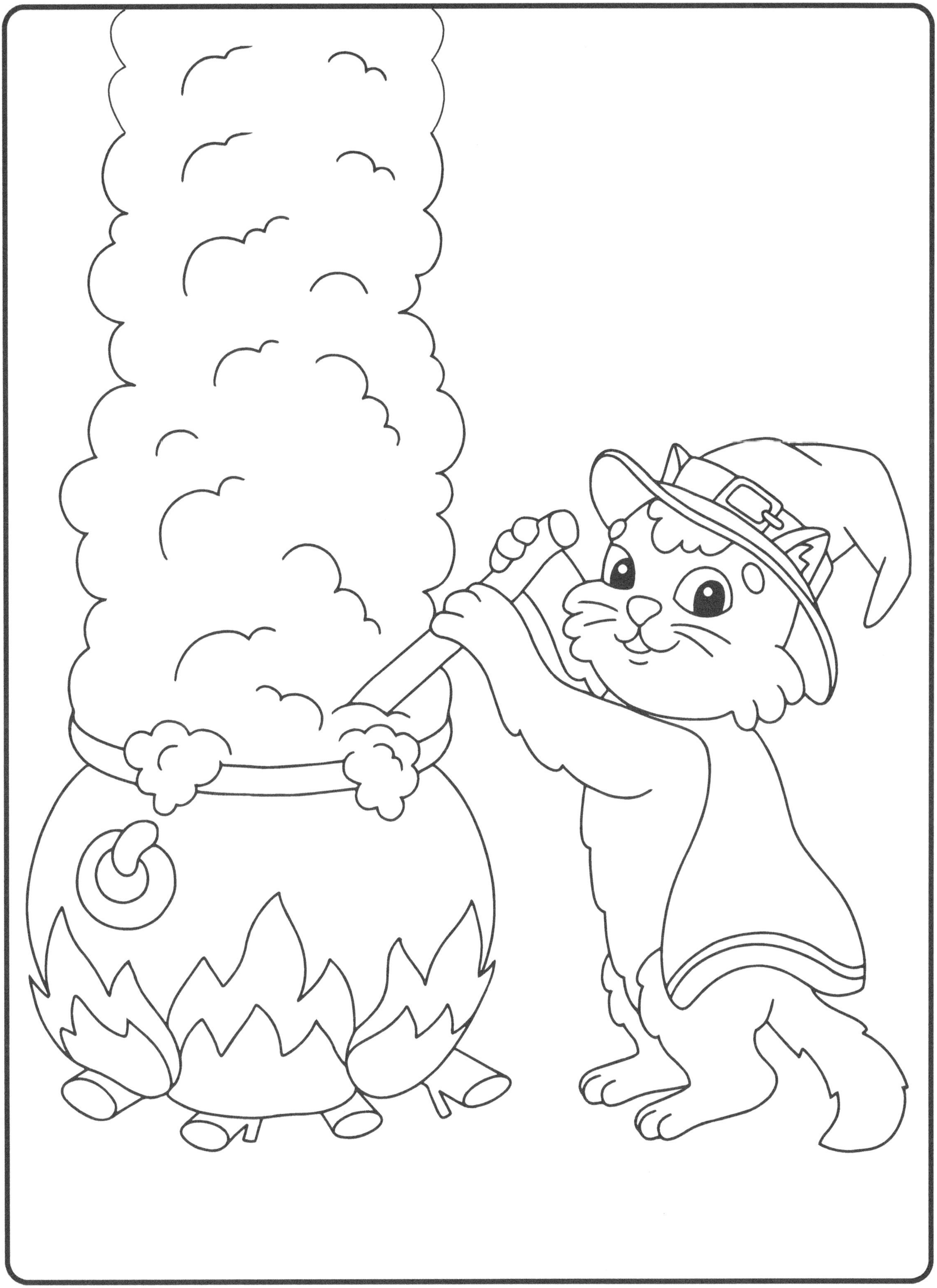

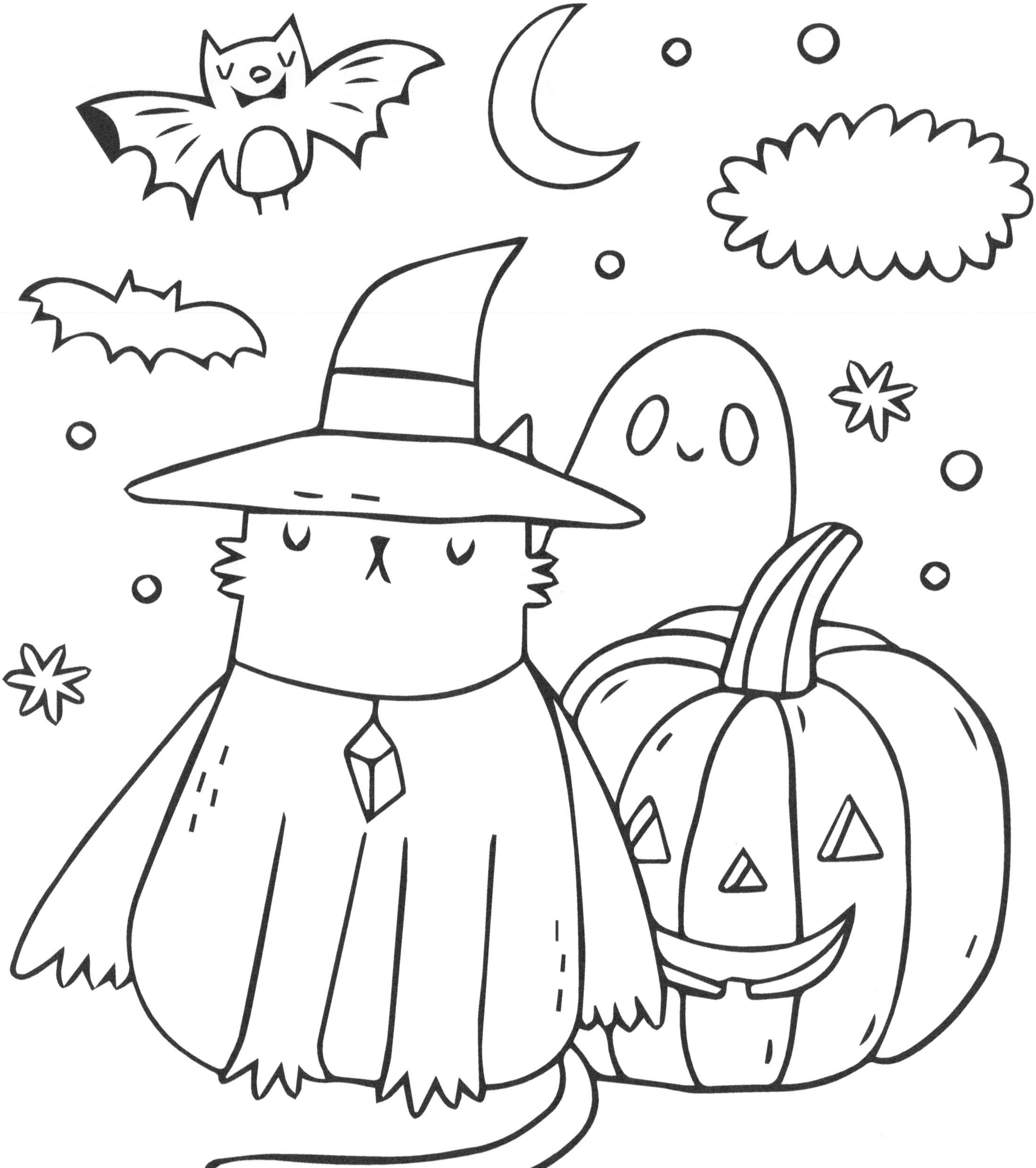

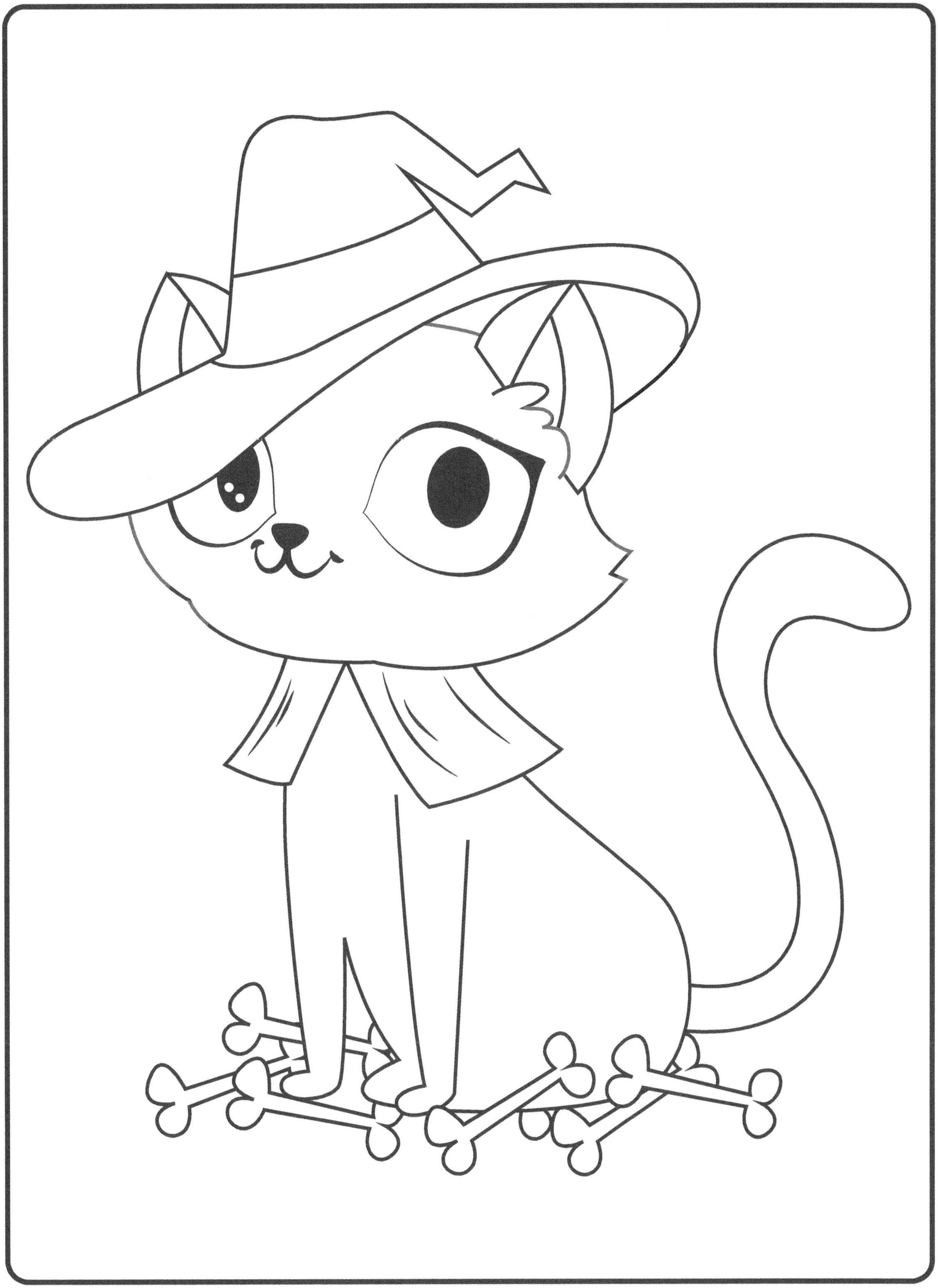

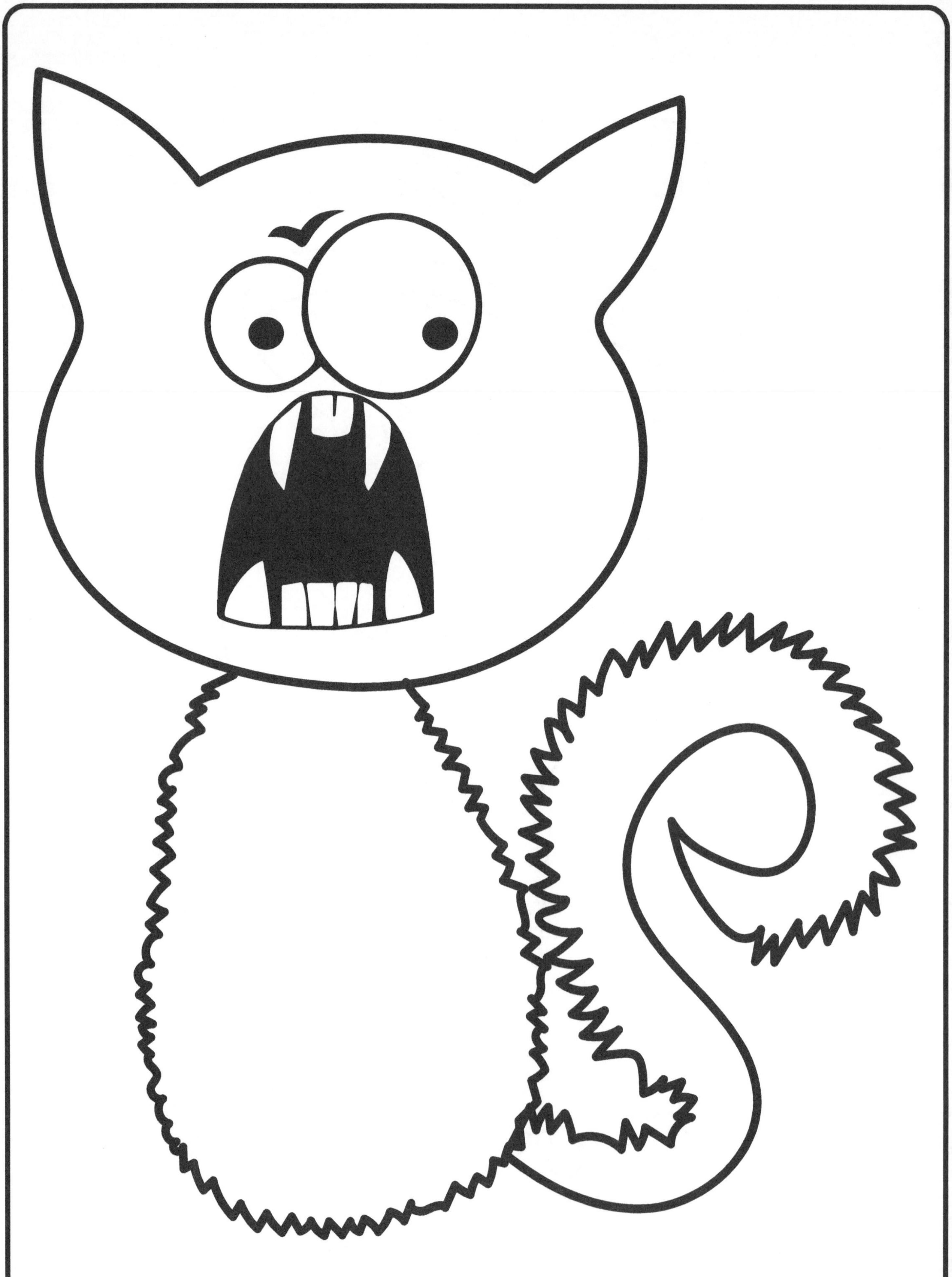

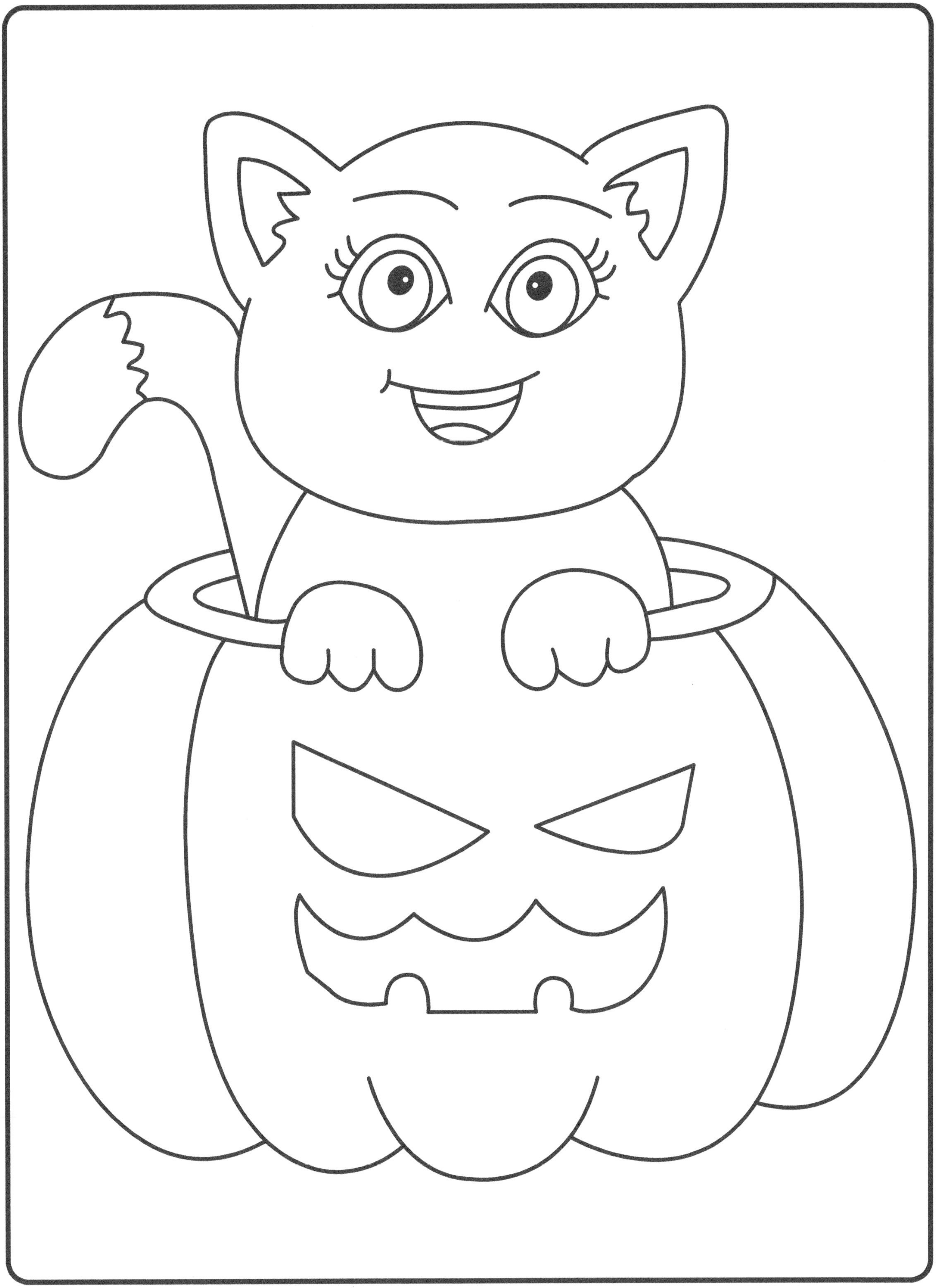

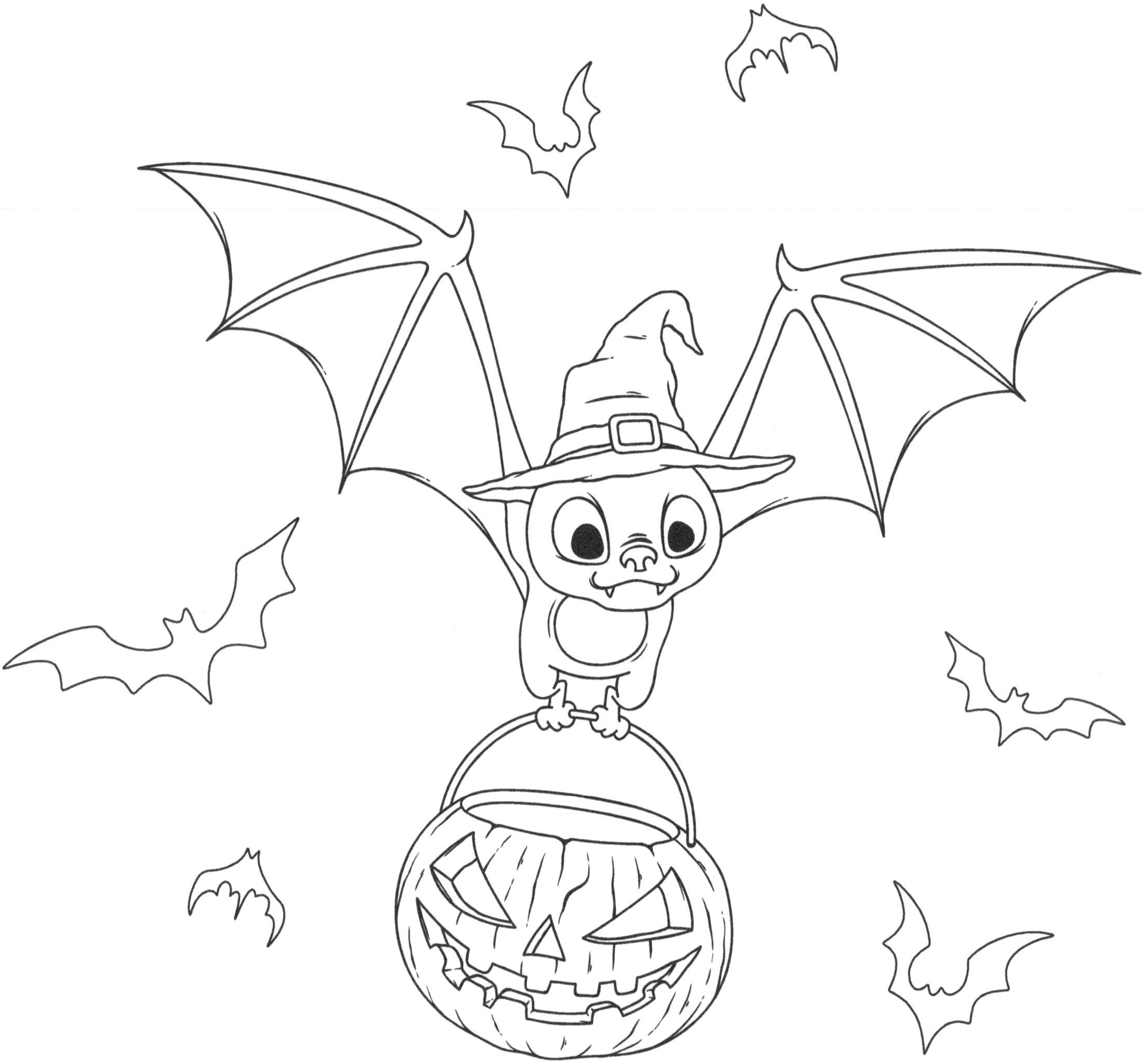

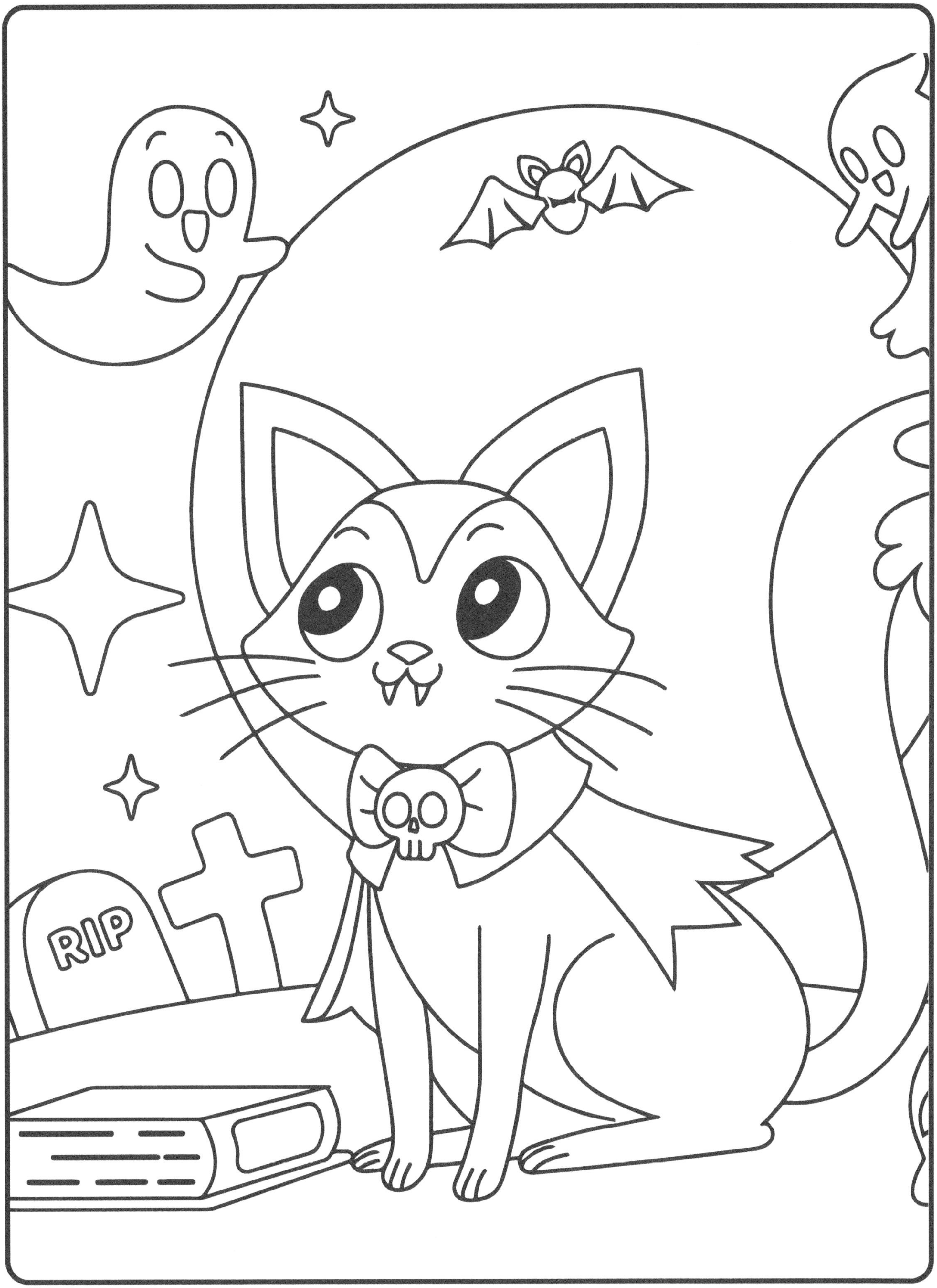
RIP

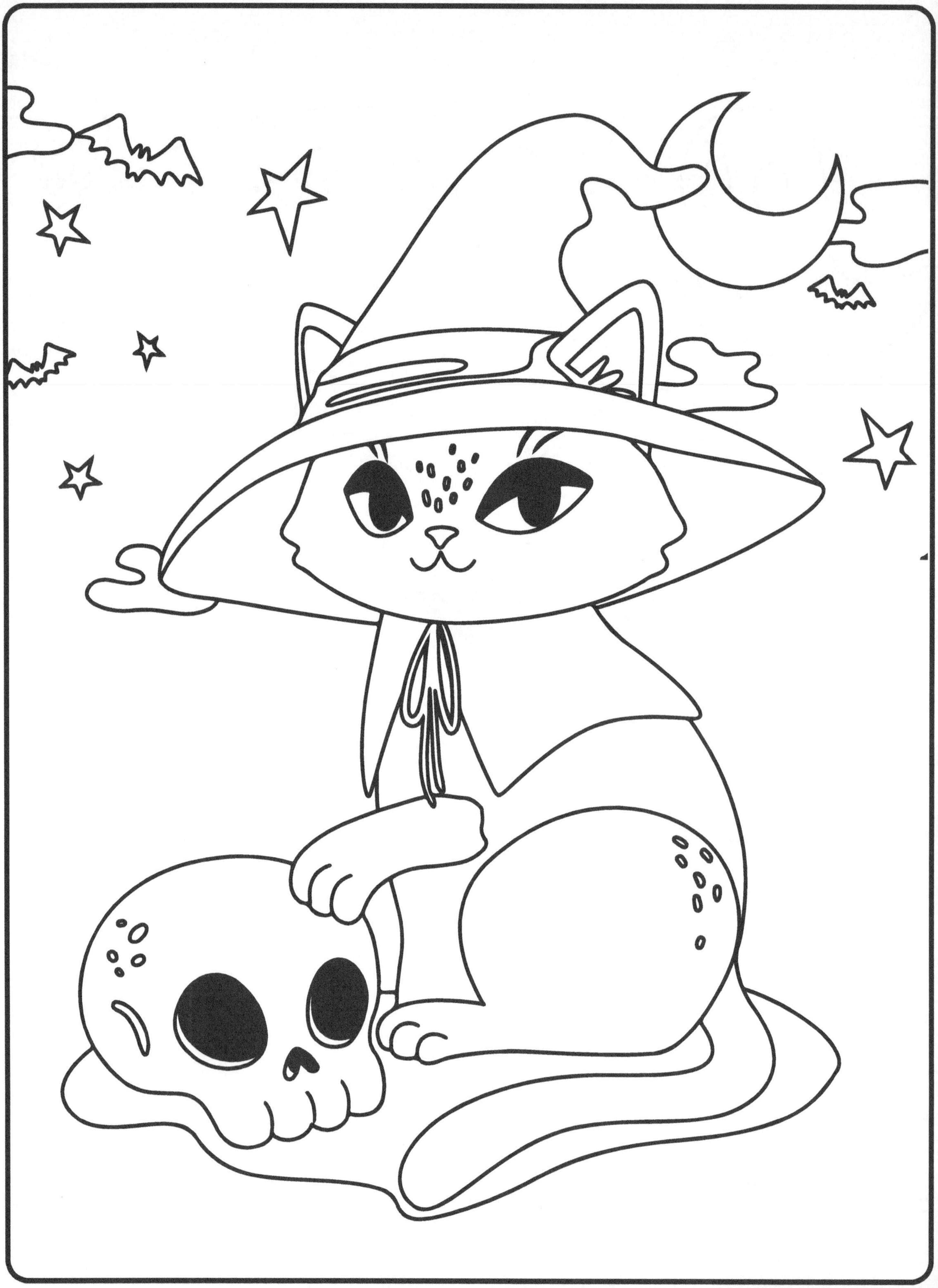

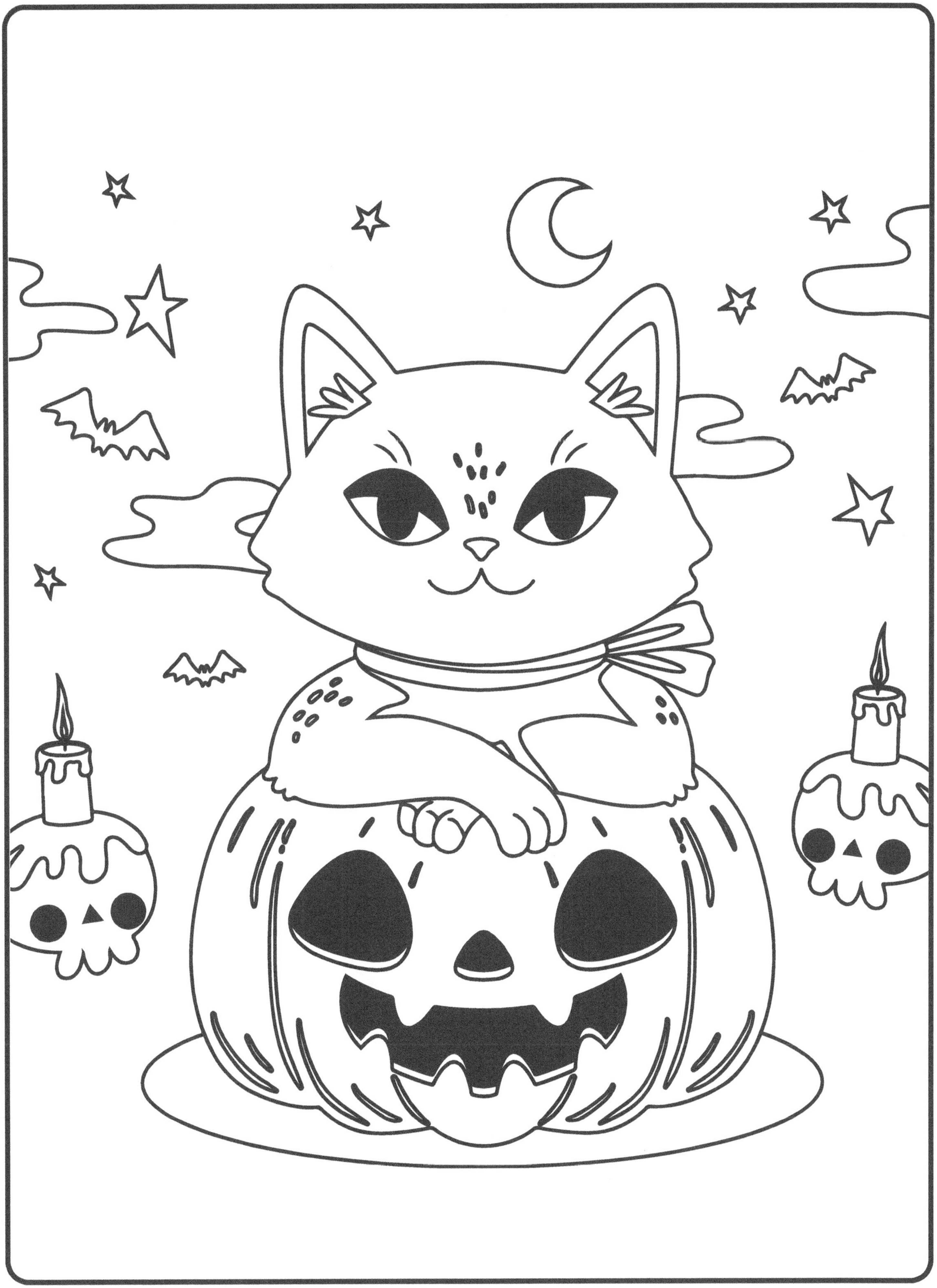

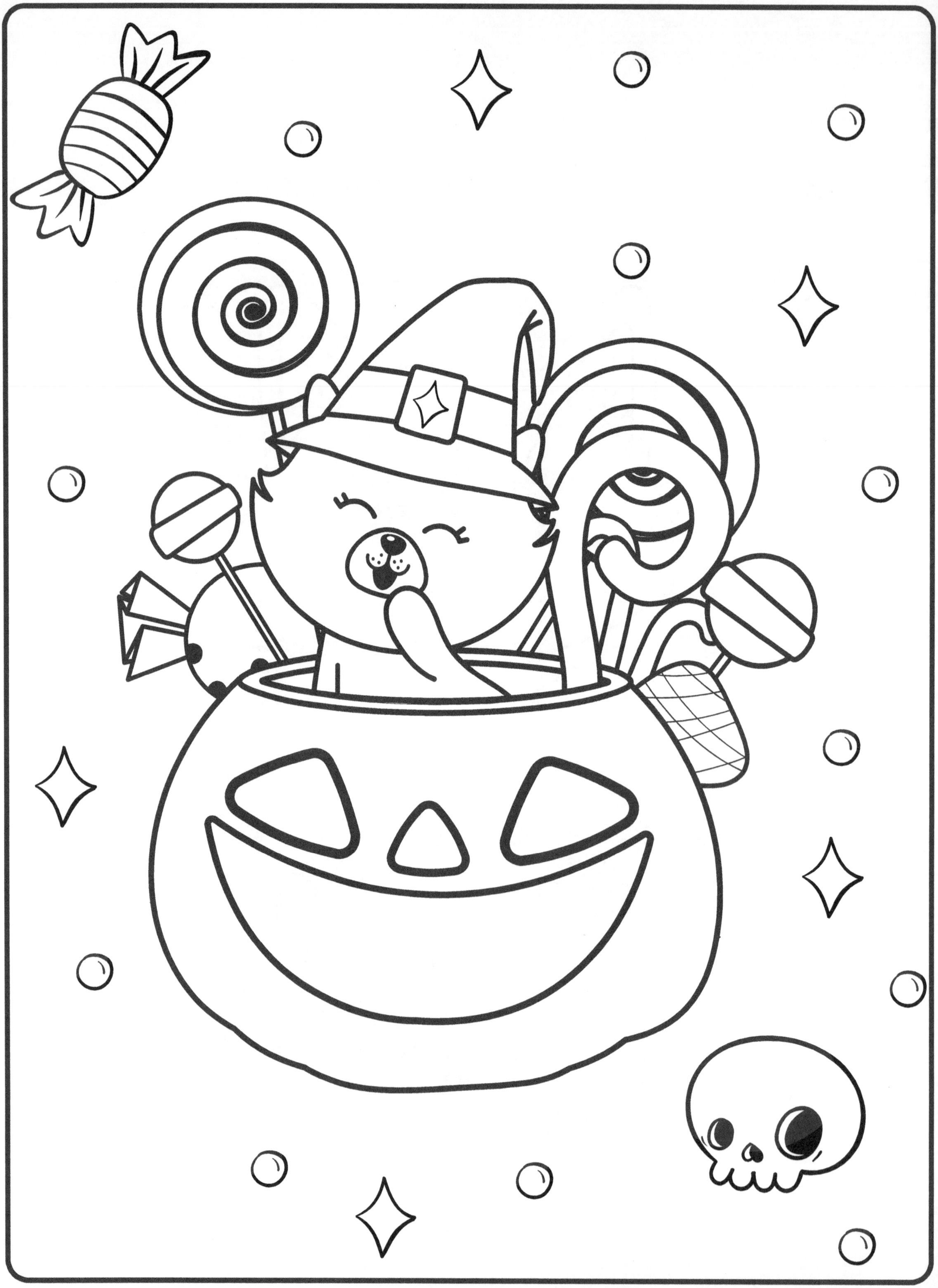

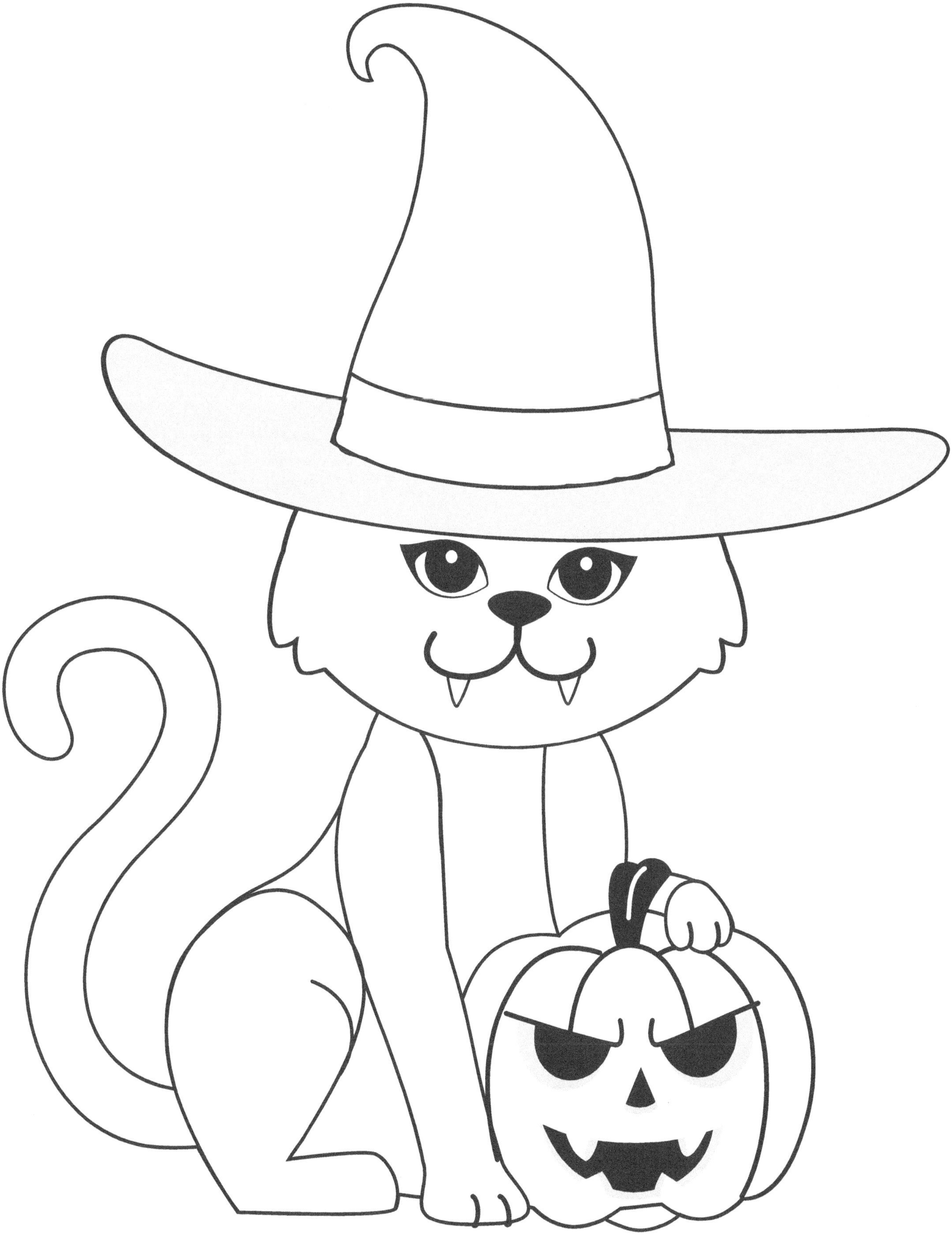

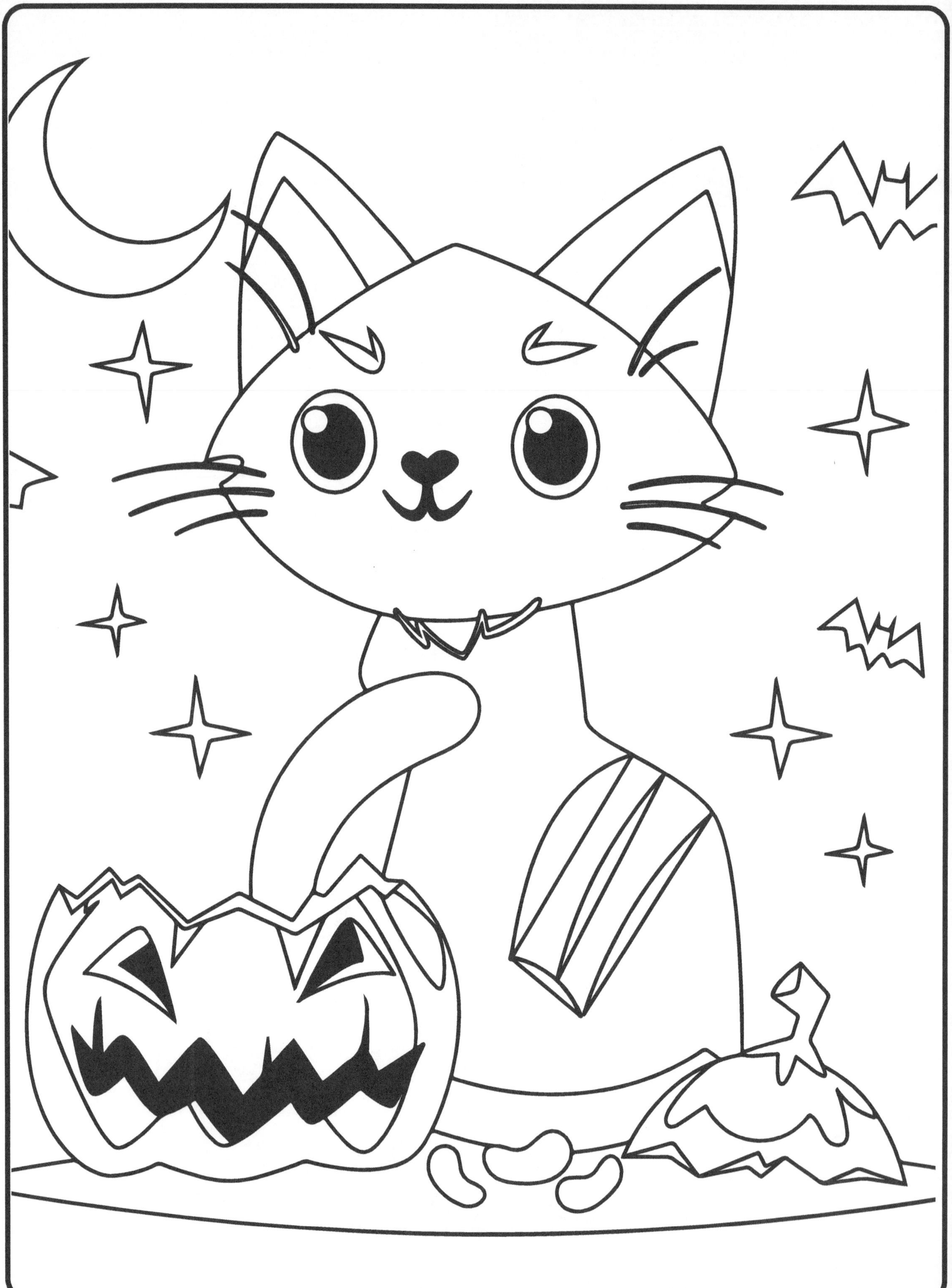

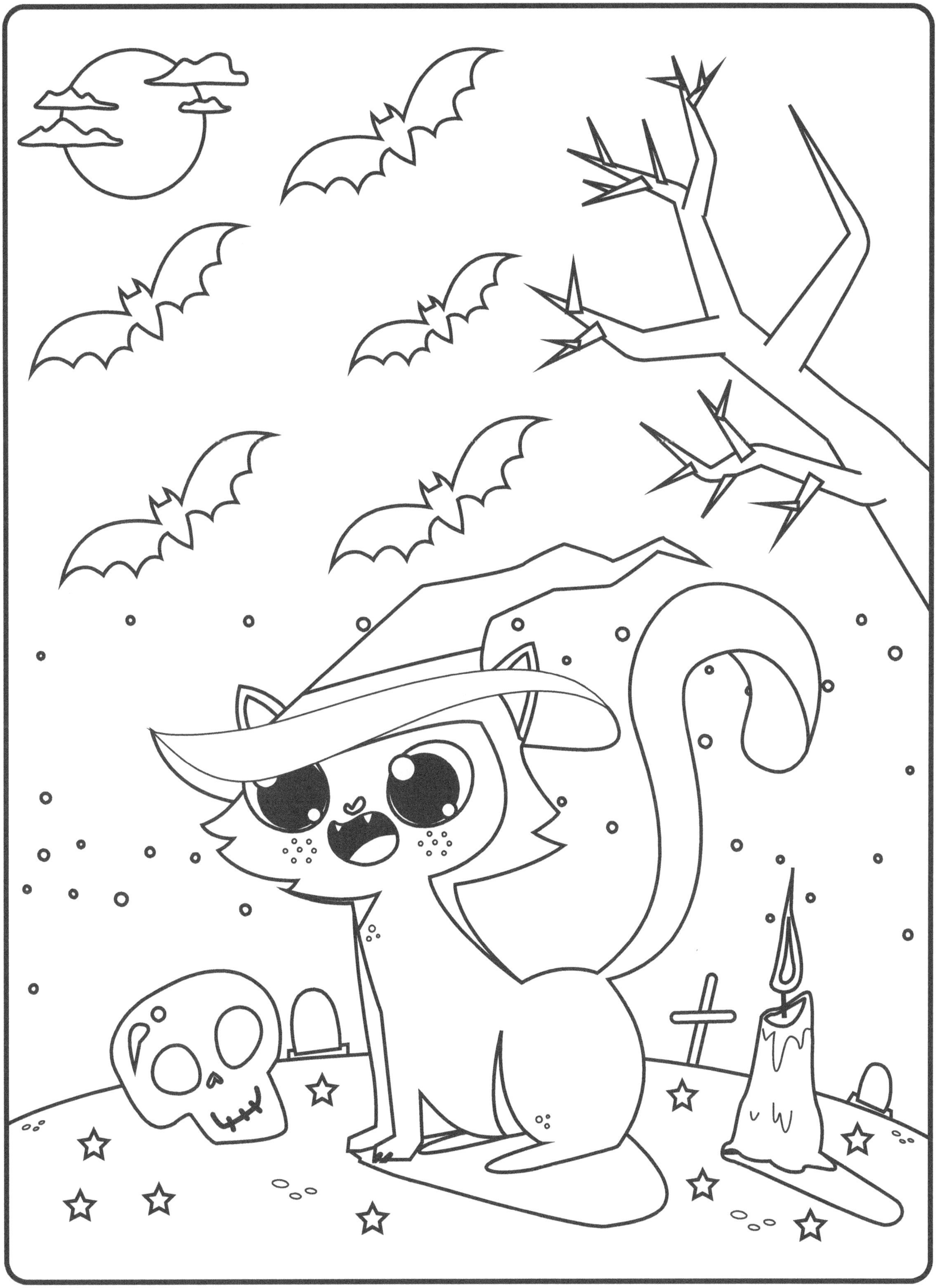

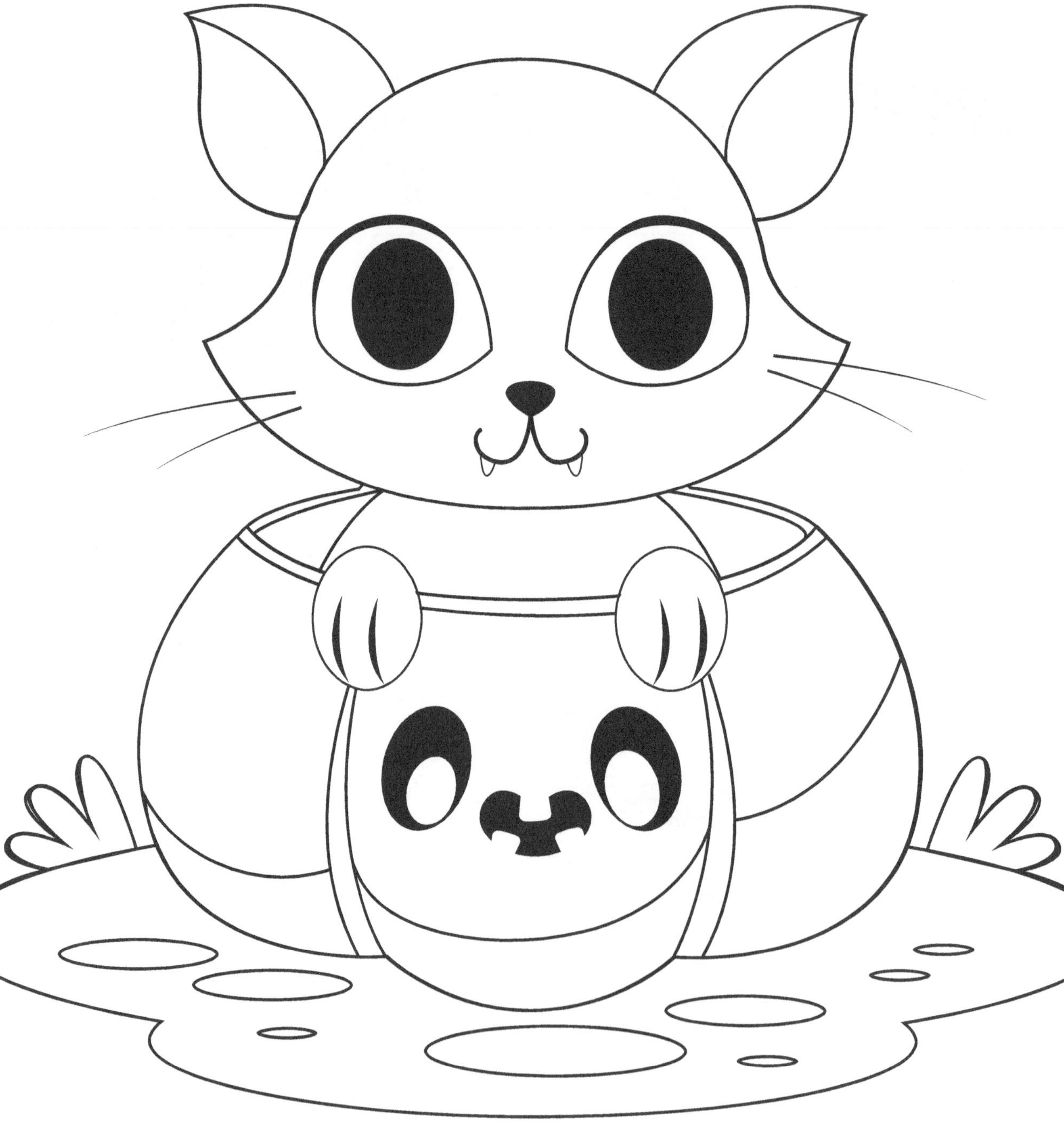

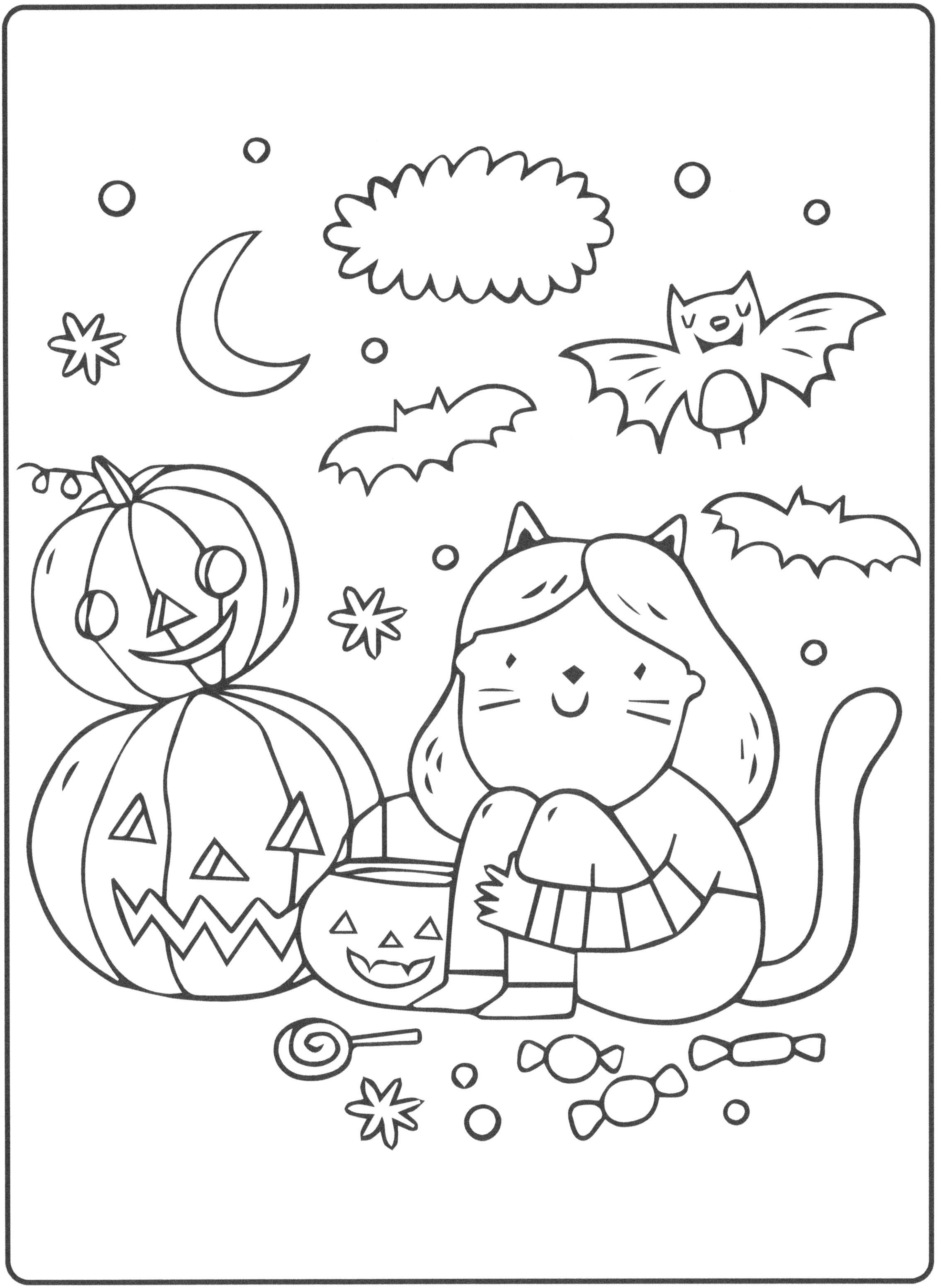

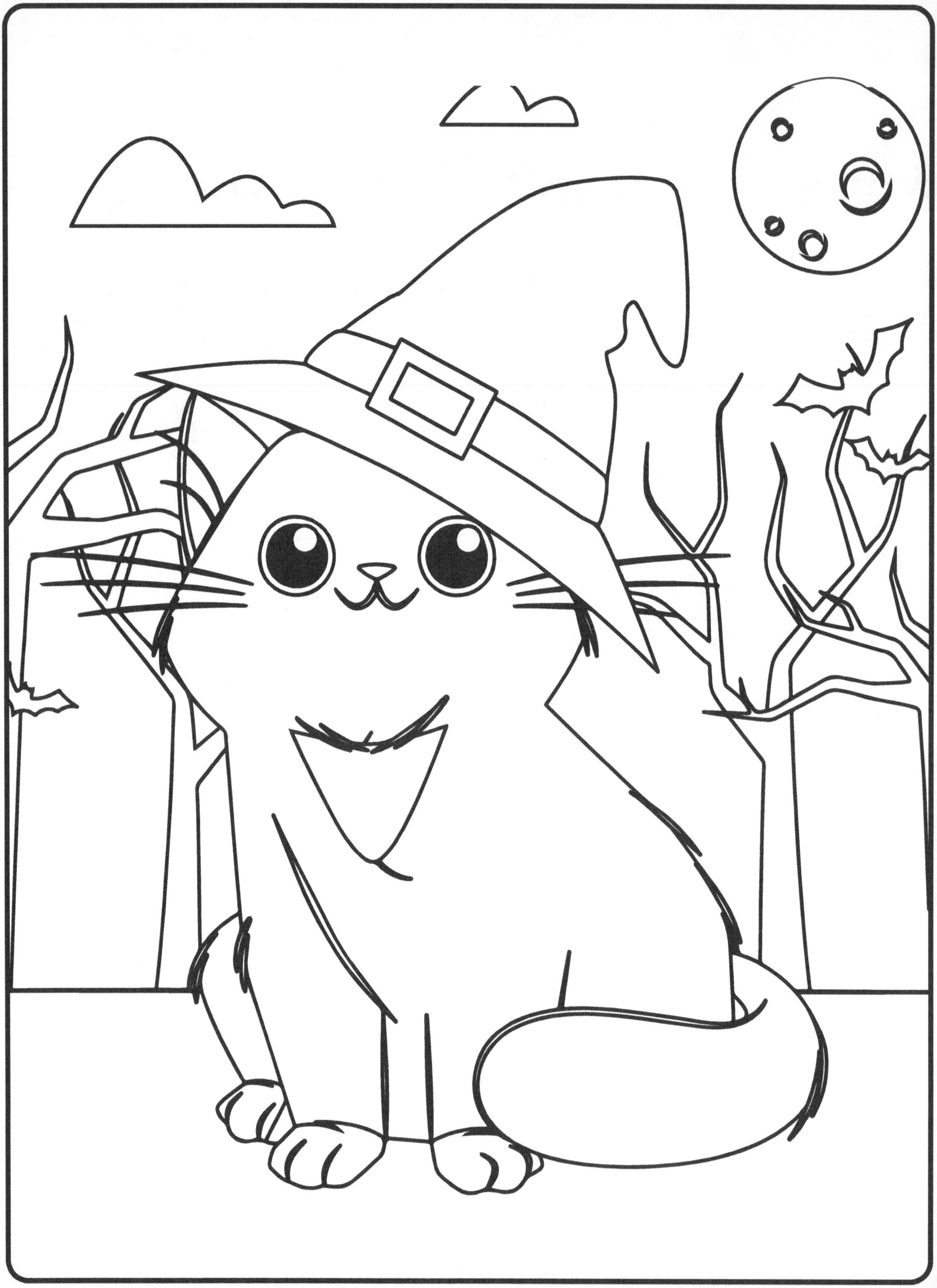

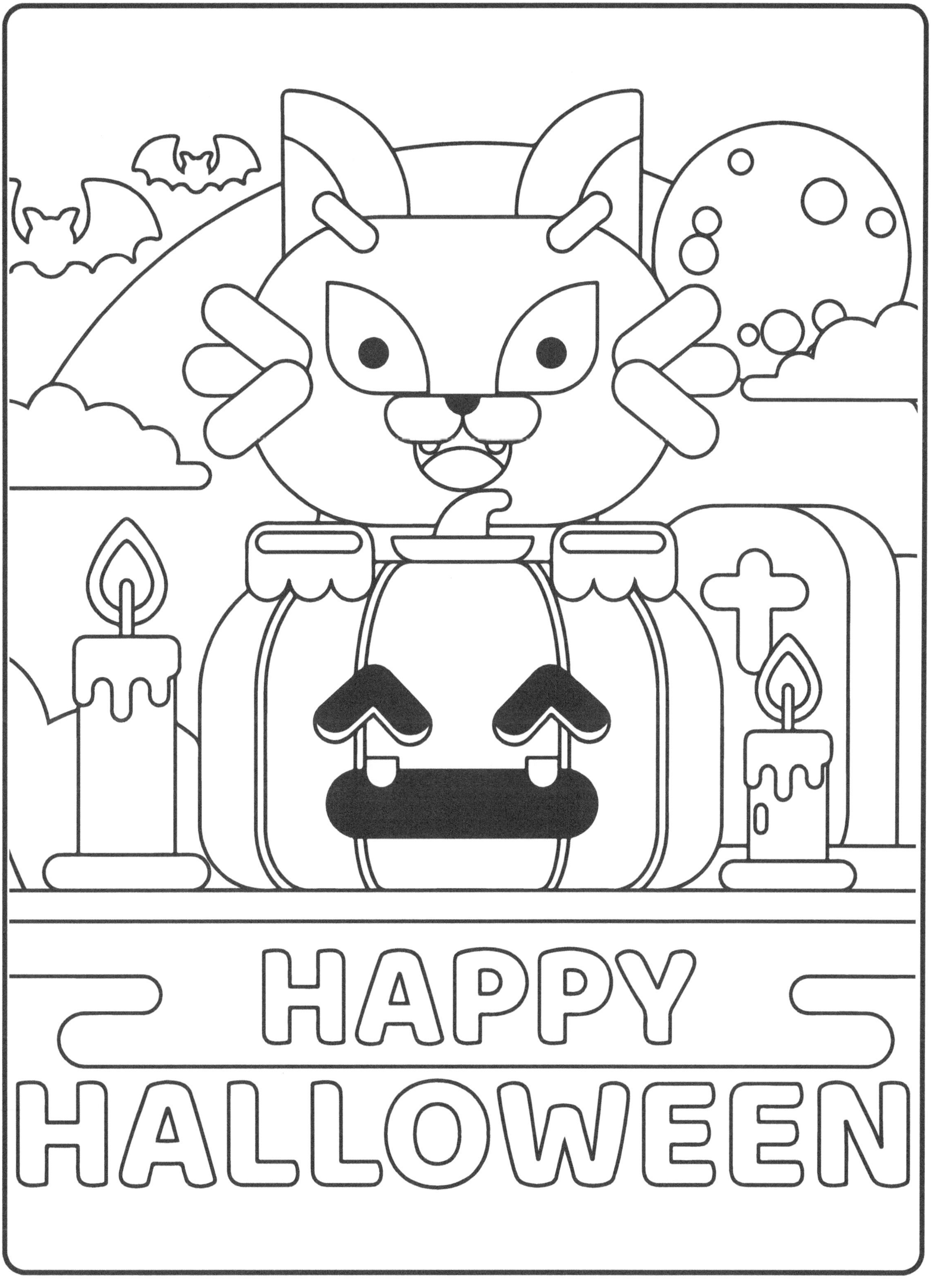
HAPPY
HALLOWEEN

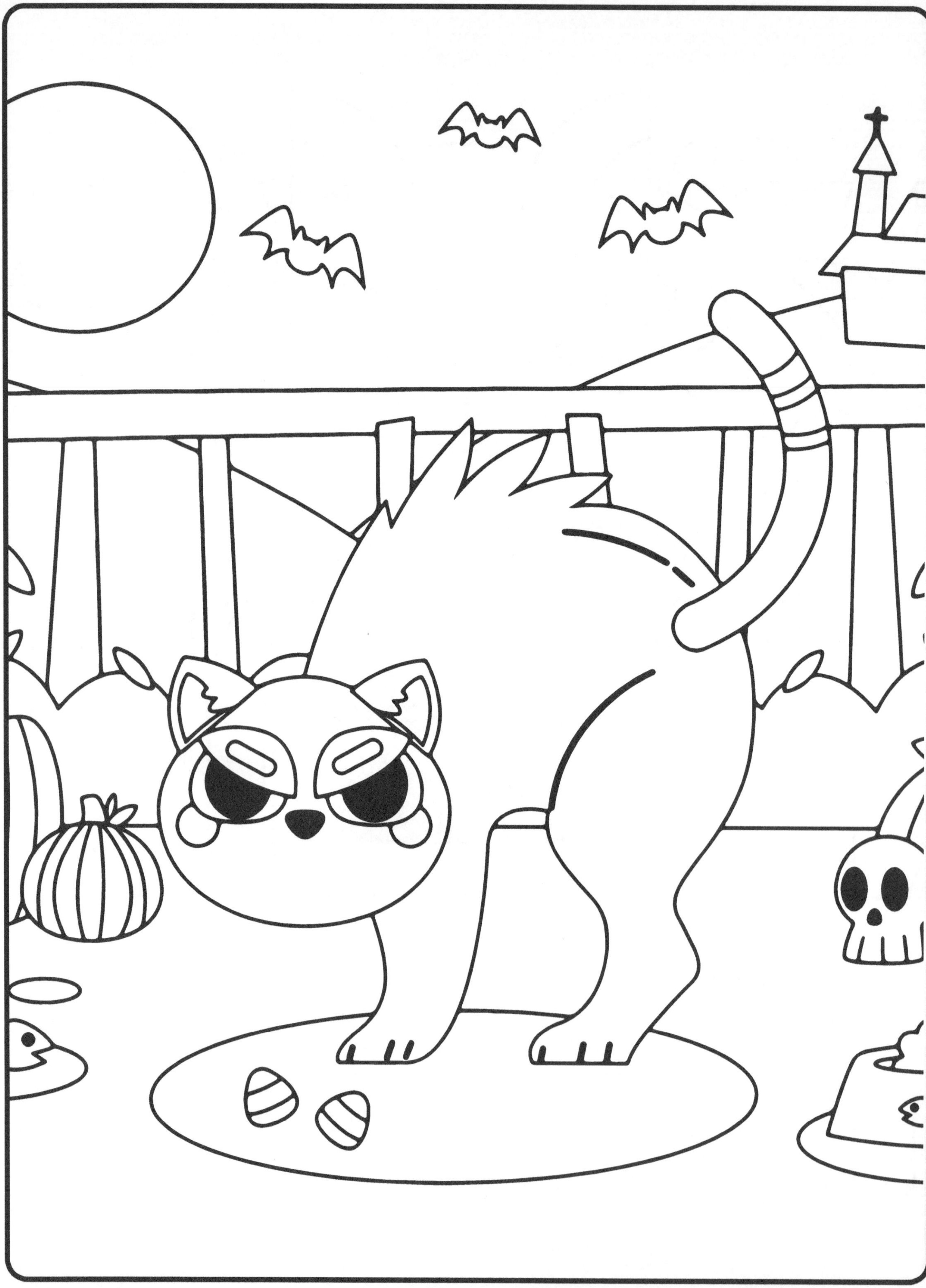

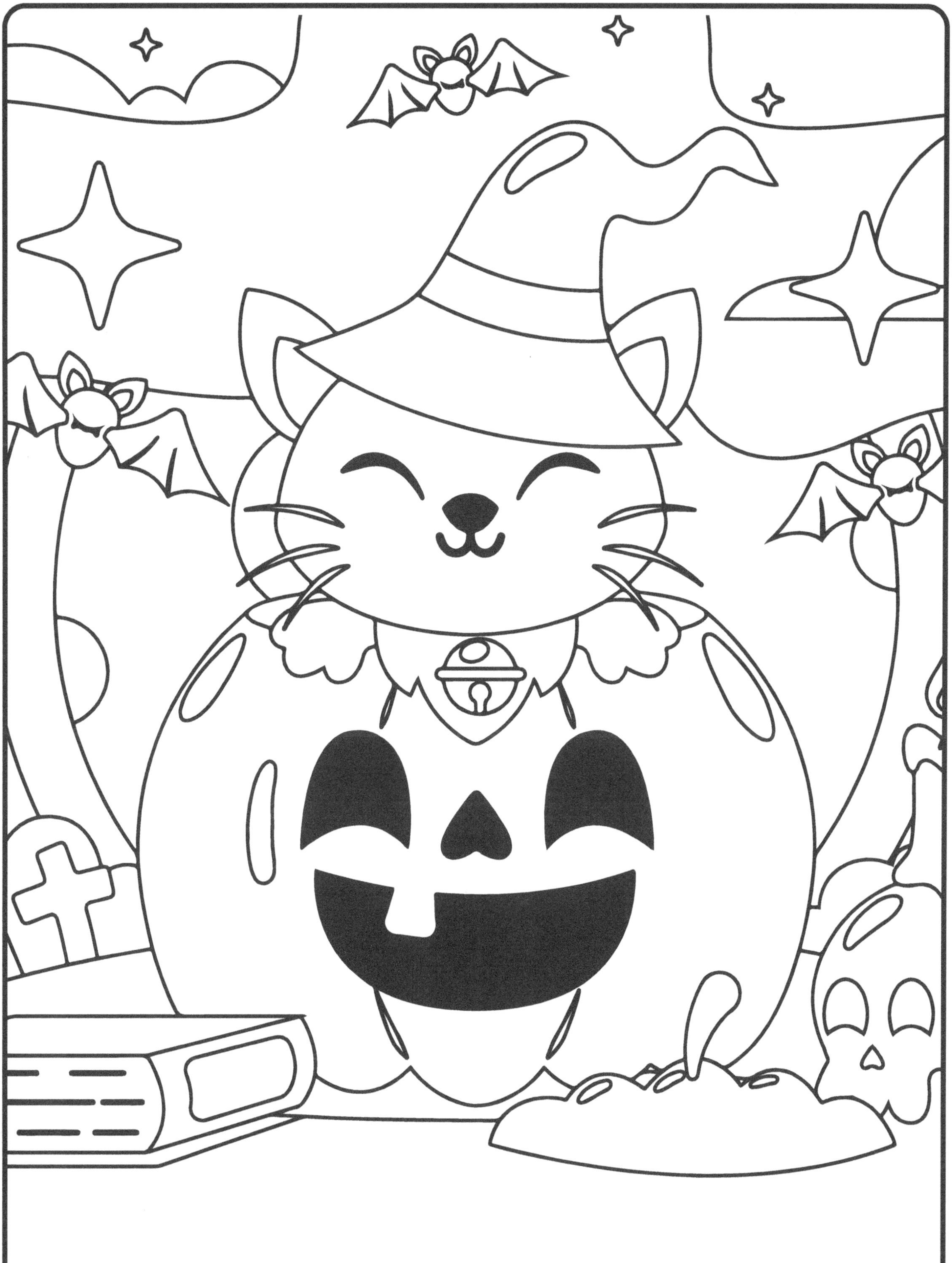

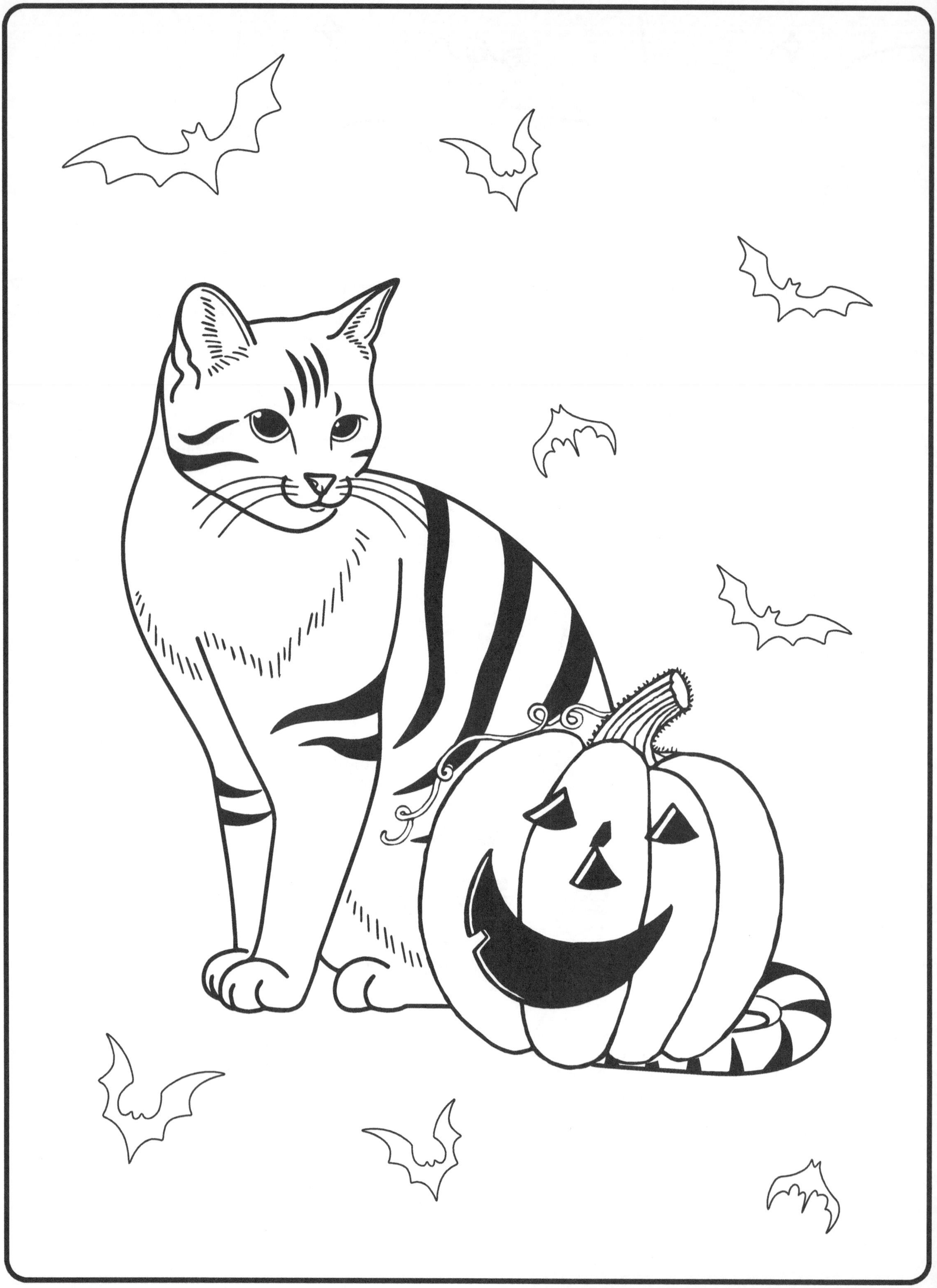

9 788194 723790

Printed at Repro India Ltd.